FIVE DIFFERENT BOOKS IN ONE COLOR-CODED FOR YOUR CONVENIENCE

- SUPERMARKET-SHOPPING GUIDE
- LOW-SODIUM-COOKING GUIDE—complete with menus, delicious recipes, flavor-magic chart, and calorie counts
- DINING-OUT GUIDE—breakfast, lunch, and dinner menus for a variety of restaurants *PLUS* A COMPLETE GUIDE TO FAST-FOOD RESTAURANTS with an item-by-item calorie and sodium count for leading fast-food chains, listed by name
- DRUGSTORE-SHOPPING GUIDE—how to avoid the hidden dangers of popular over-the-counter drugs—a complete listing with sodium content for each
- HEALTH GUIDE—a doctor answers your questions about diet and blood pressure

It's easy to put a little spice in your life with THE DELL COLOR-CODED LOW-SALT-LIVING GUIDE.

THE DELL COLOR-CODED LOW-SALT-LIVING GUIDE

Janet James and Lois Goulder

A DELL BOOK

Published by
Dell Publishing Co., Inc.
1 Dag Hammarskjold Plaza
New York, New York 10017

No copyright is claimed on material from U.S. Government publications.

Copyright © 1980 by Janet James and Lois Goulder

All rights reserved. No part of this book may be reproduced or transmitted in any form or by any means, electronic or mechanical, including photocopying, recording or by any information storage and retrieval system, without the written permission of the Publisher, except where permitted by law.

Dell ® TM 681510, Dell Publishing Co., Inc.

ISBN: 0-440-17608-5

Printed in the United States of America

First printing—June 1980
Second printing—September 1980

TABLE OF CONTENTS

PART I **THE SODIUM FACTS OF LIFE** 7

PART II **THE COLOR CODE IS THE KEY** 11

PART III **THE COLOR-CODED SUPERMARKET-SHOPPING GUIDE** 13

HOW TO USE THIS GUIDE 13
DEPARTMENTS OF THE SUPERMARKET 17

Fresh Produce 17
Fresh Meats, Poultry, Fish—Processed Meats 18
Dairy and Refrigerated Products 19
Frozen Foods 20
Cereals and Toaster Pastries 21
Canned Foods 22
Cake and Pie Mixes, Desserts, Baking Aids 23
Spaghetti, Noodles, Rice, Beans, Sauces 24
Salad Dressings, Olives, Pickles, Oils 25
Herbs and Spices 26
Packaged Bakery 27
Jellies, Ice Cream, Candy, Syrups 28
Snacks—Beverages 29

SODIUM/CALORIE COUNTER 30

PART IV **COLOR-CODED COOKING GUIDE** 66

INTRODUCTION 66
FLAVOR-MAGIC CHART 68
COMPARE AND BEWARE 70

Fresh Foods: Commercially Prepared Products 70
Green-Light Salad Dressings: Commercial Salad Dressings 71

FLAVOR-IT WITHOUT SALT 72

Low-Sodium Recipes: High-Sodium Commercial Products 73

FLAVOR-IT RECIPES 75

Sauce with Tomato Paste 75
Sauce with Fresh Tomatoes 76
Minestrone Soup 77
Swiss Steak 78
Ground Steak Belmont 79
Beef Stew 80
Taco Filling 81
Spaghetti Sauce and Meatballs 82
Spanish Rice 83
Baked Beans 84
Rump Roast 85
Herbed Meat Loaf 86
Paprika Pork Chops 86
Leg of Lamb 87
Chicken Mexican 88
Fresh Fish Broil 89

PART V A COLOR-CODED GUIDE TO DINING OUT 90

AIRLINE TRAVEL THE LOW-SODIUM WAY 91
BREAKFAST, LUNCH, AND DINNER MENUS 92
SELECT-A-SALAD AT THE SALAD BAR 96
FAST-FOOD RESTAURANTS: 97

McDonald's, Dairy Queen, Pizza Hut, Wendy's, Arby's, Kentucky Fried Chicken, Burger King

PART VI DRUGSTORE SODIUM-SHOPPING GUIDE 104

PART VII THE DOCTOR ANSWERS QUESTIONS ON SALT, BLOOD PRESSURE, AND YOUR HEALTH by Abby G. Abelson, M.D. 112

ABOUT THE AUTHORS 123

BIBLIOGRAPHY 124

MEDICAL BIBLIOGRAPHY 125

PART I

THE SODIUM FACTS OF LIFE: YOU CAN IMPROVE YOUR HEALTH IF YOU EAT LESS SALT!

That was the conclusion of the U.S. Senate Select Committee on Nutrition and Human Needs after hearing health and nutrition experts from all over the country testify that there is a link between salt intake and blood pressure. In their 1977 report, *Dietary Goals for the United States*, the Committee advised eating less salt as an "important countermeasure" to high blood pressure.

High blood pressure is a major health problem that affects nearly thirty-five million Americans and threatens an additional twenty-five million more who have borderline high blood pressure. This means that sixty million Americans—one out of every four—face increased risk of heart attack and stroke, which claim hundreds of thousands of victims every year. That is why, when setting down nutrition guidelines for Americans to follow, the Committee concluded that Americans should EAT LESS SALT. Other leading health authorities support this conclusion.

EATING LESS SALT MEANS EATING LESS SODIUM, because salt is a chemical compound known as sodium chloride. Ordinary table salt is thirty-nine percent sodium. It is the sodium in salt that may affect blood pressure in some people by changing the body's fluid balance. An intake of too much sodium may result in too much fluid accumulating in the body. The excess fluid exerts a greater push against the walls of the blood vessels, creating a higher blood pressure and a potentially dangerous health risk.

To reduce this health risk many doctors recommend a specific diet based on individual needs. The doctor or dietitian may refer to this diet as "low salt" or "low sodium." Either of these terms is correct.

The American Heart Association shares the concern of the U.S. Senate Select Committee as to the amount of salt Americans consume. Its 1978 report on *Diet and Coronary Heart Disease* states that "it is prudent to avoid excessive sodium in the diet." The term "excessive sodium" means too much salt.

How much is too much? The Senate report found that Americans consume between 6,000 and 18,000 milligrams of salt per day. The report recommends REDUCING SALT INTAKE to "about 5,000 milligrams a day"—far less than the amount now consumed by the average American. If we were to follow the Senate Committee's advice it would mean a dramatic reduction in our daily salt intake and a step on the road to better health for all of us.

The *Dietary Goals* recommendation to reduce salt intake to 5,000 milligrams a day means that we should reduce sodium intake to about 2,000 milligrams a day.

But Americans now consume from 2,400 to 7,200 milligrams of sodium a day. So the person even in the lowest range of consumption is eating more sodium than the amount recommended by *Dietary Goals*.

HERE IS WHAT AMERICANS EAT PER DAY:
(estimated range)

HIGHEST CONSUMPTION OF SODIUM
7,200 mgs. of sodium   (in 3½ teaspoons of salt)

LOWEST CONSUMPTION OF SODIUM
2,400 mgs. of sodium   (in slightly more than 1 teaspoon of salt)

HERE IS WHAT AMERICANS SHOULD EAT PER DAY:
(*Dietary Goals* Recommendation)

2,000 mgs. of sodium   (in slightly less than 1 teaspoon of salt)

These figures show that there is a significant gap between the amount of sodium we are now eating, and the amount we should be eating. How can we bridge this gap? How can we reduce the amount of sodium that we consume every day?

Well, we can throw away the salt shaker. We can stop adding salt to the foods we cook, and we can stop sprinkling it over everything we eat at the table. And that will really help lessen the amount of sodium in our daily diet.

But we can't eliminate all the sodium in our diet by

throwing away the salt shaker, because *sodium is in almost everything we eat.* It's found in nearly all the plant and animal sources we use as foods. It's in meats and dairy products and—usually in smaller amounts—in vegetables and fruits. It's also added for flavor to commercially prepared food products.

Practically every food that we eat contains some sodium. So most of us consume the recommended 2,000 mgs. of sodium a day in the foods of a well-balanced diet WITHOUT ADDING ANY SALT during cooking or at the table. And it's even in some drugstore products—over-the-counter remedies that we buy without a doctor's prescription.

So if you want to improve your health, use this LOW-SALT-LIVING GUIDE to help you follow the recommendations of the *Dietary Goals* and the American Heart Association to cut down the amount of sodium you consume daily.

The LOW-SALT-LIVING GUIDE is FIVE GUIDES IN ONE:

1. SUPERMARKET-SHOPPING GUIDE
2. LOW-SODIUM-COOKING GUIDE
3. DINING-OUT GUIDE (including Fast-Food Restaurants)
4. DRUGSTORE-SHOPPING GUIDE
5. HEALTH GUIDE: A Doctor Answers Questions on Diet and Blood Pressure

PART II
THE COLOR CODE IS THE KEY

As a nutritionist and author of two cookbooks, Janet James was often asked for help with special health problems related to foods. She was frequently asked the following questions:

"How can I stay on a low salt diet if I don't know which foods are lower in salt?"

"How can I make foods tasty without adding salt?"

"Is there anything I can eat at a restaurant that's low in salt?"

Ms. James knew that she couldn't answer any questions about salt without discussing sodium, because ordinary table salt contains thirty-nine percent sodium. She also knew that researching the sodium contents of all the foods in the American diet would be a long and difficult task.

She asked Lois Goulder for help. Together they began a search that led them to consult with physicians, university nutritionists, nurses, food editors, and hospital dietitians. They turned to the Department of Agriculture for their latest data. Food manufacturers were consulted for information on the sodium contents of their products.

The leading fast-food restaurant chains were contacted for their latest nutritional information. Biomedical experts and pharmacists researched the sodium content of over-the-counter drugs. Physicians were consulted for information relating salt (sodium) intake to high blood pressure.

After completing their extensive research, the authors realized they needed a way to change the complicated nutritional data into a simple form that was easy to understand. So they devised a unique COLOR CODE, which became the key to the LOW-SALT-LIVING GUIDE.

The colors from the traffic signal were chosen, because everyone knows what they mean. These colors were applied to the sodium content of foods:

> GREEN IS GO—for better health
> GREEN means the foods are LOW IN SODIUM

> YELLOW IS CAUTION
> YELLOW means the foods are MODERATE IN SODIUM

> RED IS STOP—DANGER
> RED means the foods are HIGH IN SODIUM

The color code is also the key to a companion guide to better health, written by the same authors. THE DELL COLOR-CODED LOW-FAT-LIVING GUIDE will help you to cut down on the amount of saturated fat and cholesterol in your diet. Special features include: the low-fat supermarket-shopping guide; guide to losing weight; dining-out guide (including fast-food restaurants); low-fat recipes that are also low in salt; and medical information on diet and coronary heart disease. In both of these books the color code will brighten your way to healthier eating.

PART III

THE COLOR-CODED SUPERMARKET-SHOPPING GUIDE

HOW TO USE THIS GUIDE

AT HOME
to plan your low-sodium meals.

AT THE SUPERMARKET
to choose your low-sodium foods.

WHEN CONSULTING WITH YOUR DOCTOR OR DIETITIAN
if you are on a sodium-restricted diet.

This shopping guide will lead you through the supermarket, with a separate COLOR-CODED PAGE for each department. On each page the foods are classified BY COLOR, according to the sodium content of each food listed.

To make your choices, consult the Table of Contents at the front of the book for the page of the Supermarket Guide which lists the foods in that particular department.

THE COLOR CODE MAKES IT EASY TO CHOOSE:

> The foods listed in GREEN are
> LOW IN SODIUM CONTENT

> The foods listed in YELLOW are
> MODERATE IN SODIUM CONTENT

> The foods listed in RED are
> HIGH IN SODIUM CONTENT

The color code will help you make healthier food choices at the supermarket. The foods are *color coded within each department of the supermarket,* according to their relative sodium content. Sodium is measured in milligrams.

As an example, if you are shopping for dairy products, turn to page 19 of the Supermarket Guide for the Dairy Department.

Which cottage cheese should you buy—dry cottage cheese or creamed cottage cheese? The color code immediately makes it clear. You should buy dry cottage cheese listed in GREEN, rather than creamed cottage cheese listed in RED.

If you want to know the exact sodium content of these products, turn to page 37 of the sodium/calorie counter, which lists the foods in the Dairy Department. You will quickly find the color-coded listing:

> Cottage cheese, dry . . ½ cup . . 14 mgs. of sodium

> Cottage cheese, creamed . . ½ cup . . 457 mgs. of sodium

You will note that cottage cheese is in ½ cup servings, considered to be the *usual serving size*. The sodium/calorie counter lists all foods according to the amount of sodium found in a *usual serving* of a particular food.

The color code applies *only* to the serving size listed in the sodium/calorie counter.

The sodium/calorie counter is organized like the shopping guide, according to each department of the supermarket. Each food is coded in the same color as it is in the Supermarket-Shopping Guide.

If a food is not listed in this Supermarket Guide, read the product label carefully to determine if salt or sodium is listed as an ingredient. Remember that a food label lists ingredients in order of quantity, with the first ingredient largest in quantity, and the rest following in diminishing order.

The food industry has been cooperating with the U.S. Food and Drug Administration by adding nutrition information about their products on the package label. Some manufacturers already list the sodium content, in milligrams, on their labels, and many more products will include this information in the future.

Even though the sodium content is not listed on a product, a manufacturer may state on the label "NO SALT ADDED" or "UNSALTED."

This guide includes only those foods for which authoritative data on sodium content are available. The sources of this data are listed in the Bibliography on page 135. Some figures for sodium content and calories were obtained from individual food manufacturers, and are designated with an asterisk (*) in the sodium/calorie counter.

THE COLOR-CODED SUPERMARKET-SHOPPING GUIDE was prepared with the assistance of Grace J. Petot, M.S., R.D., Assistant Professor, Department of Nutrition, Case Western Reserve University. She also volunteers professional services to the American Heart Association.

DEPARTMENTS OF THE SUPERMARKET

FRESH PRODUCE

ALL FRESH FRUITS

DRIED FRUITS

ALL FRESH VEGETABLES

UNSALTED NUTS

FRESH ORANGE JUICE

FRESH GRAPEFRUIT JUICE

See the Flavor-Magic Chart on pages 68 and 69 for new ways to season vegetables without salt. Add variety to your salads with the Green-Light Salad Dressings on page 71.

FRESH MEATS, POULTRY, FISH— PROCESSED MEATS

FRESH BEEF, LAMB, PORK, AND VEAL

FRESH POULTRY:
- CHICKEN
- TURKEY

FRESH FISH (WHOLE, or FILLET from WHOLE FRESH FISH):

- COD
- HADDOCK
- HALIBUT
- OYSTERS
- PERCH
- PIKE
- SALMON
- SNAPPER
- SOLE

- LOBSTER
- SCALLOPS
- SHRIMP
- BEEF KIDNEYS

HAM (CURED)   CANNED HAM

ALL PROCESSED MEATS:

- BACON
- CANADIAN BACON
- DRIED BEEF
- BOLOGNA
- FRANKFURTERS
- CHOPPED HAM
- HAM LOAF
- LIVERWURST
- SAUSAGE
- SALAMI

SAUERKRAUT

DAIRY AND REFRIGERATED PRODUCTS

SWEET BUTTER SWEET-UNSALTED
COFFEE CREAM MARGARINE
HALF-AND-HALF SOUR CREAM
  CREAM WHIPPING CREAM
IMITATION SOUR CREAM (nondairy)
CHEESE: cottage cheese (dry; no salt added),
        cream cheese, Neufchatel, Gruyère
MILK: Skim milk Whole milk
    Low-fat milk, 1% Low-fat milk, 2%
    Chocolate milk (whole, low-fat 1% and 2%)
LOW-FAT YOGURT (plain and fruit-flavored)
WHIPPED CREAM TOPPING (pressurized)
EGGS EGGNOG HORSERADISH*

CHEESE: brick, cheddar, Colby, Monterey Jack,
       mozzarella (low moisture, part-skim),
       ricotta (part-skim)
BUTTER (SALTED) MARGARINE
                        (SALTED)
REFRIGERATED COOKIE DOUGH

BUTTERMILK
CHEESE: American, Blue, Camembert, Edam,
       Feta, Gouda, Parmesan, Roquefort,
       Swiss
CREAMED COTTAGE CHEESE—4% or 6%
COTTAGE CHEESE—LOW-FAT 1% or 2%
SALT IS ADDED to Creamed Cottage Cheese
and Low-fat Cottage Cheese
HERRING
SMOKED SALMON
DILL PICKLES

*Some manufacturers add salt. Read the ingredient list on the label.

FROZEN FOODS

ALL FROZEN FRUITS
ALL FROZEN FRUIT JUICES
ALL FROZEN VEGETABLES (PLAIN)
COFFEE WHITENER (nondairy)
DESSERT TOPPING (nondairy)
(pressurized and semisolid)

FROZEN VEGETABLES WITH SAUCES
 are always higher in sodium content than PLAIN frozen vegetables. Use the sodium/calorie counter at the back of this Supermarket Guide to compare the sodium content of plain frozen vegetables with frozen vegetables with sauces.
FROZEN WHOLE TURKEY
FROZEN FISH
 Sodium preservatives frequently are used to process frozen fish.
FROZEN EGG SUBSTITUTES
FROZEN DOUGHNUTS—BLUEBERRY
                                MUFFINS
FROZEN ROLLS
FROZEN CHOCOLATE BROWNIE

FROZEN TURKEY ROLL
CHICKEN AND TURKEY POT PIES
MEAT POT PIES
ALL FROZEN MAIN DISH "TV DINNERS"
FROZEN FRIED FISH
FROZEN WAFFLES
FROZEN CORN MUFFINS
FROZEN CAKES
FROZEN PIES
FROZEN PIZZA

CEREALS AND TOASTER PASTRIES

READY-TO-EAT CEREALS:

SHREDDED WHEAT
PUFFED WHEAT (plain)
PUFFED RICE (plain)

HOT CEREALS*: (Prepared *Without Salt*)

RICE CEREAL
WHEAT CEREALS:
   Cracked Wheat
   Rolled Wheat
   Malted Wheat
OAT CEREALS

WHEAT GERM

CORN MEAL (Yellow and White) Enriched

ALL READY-TO-EAT CEREALS *EXCEPT* THOSE LISTED ABOVE

"NATURAL" CEREALS
TOASTER PASTRIES
BREAKFAST BARS

*Some cereals are higher in sodium content than others. Check the SODIUM/CALORIE COUNTER following this Shopping Guide for sodium content of individual cereals.

INSTANT CEREALS WITH IMITATION BACON OR HAM
CORN MEAL (Self-Rising)

CANNED FOODS
FRUITS AND JUICES, VEGETABLES, SOUPS, FISH, MEATS, READY-TO-SERVE FOODS, CHINESE FOODS

ALL CANNED FRUITS

ALL FRUIT JUICES

CANNED SWEET POTATOES

CANNED VEGETABLES:
  asparagus, beets, carrots, corn, green beans, lima beans, peas, spinach, tomatoes, yellow beans

  Look for labels which say "NO SALT ADDED" on canned vegetables.

CANNED VEGETABLE JUICES

CANNED SHRIMP

CANNED MUSHROOMS

CANNED SAUERKRAUT

CANNED FISH (crab, salmon, sardines, tuna)

CANNED MEATS

ALL CANNED SOUPS, DEHYDRATED SOUPS, BOUILLON CUBES

READY-TO-SERVE MAIN DISHES

CANNED SPAGHETTI AND MACARONI

CHINESE DINNERS—SOY SAUCE

See special DIETETIC FOODS SECTION for Low-Sodium Canned Foods.

CAKE AND PIE MIXES, DESSERTS, BAKING AIDS

CHOCOLATE (baking, bitter, semisweet)
FLOUR (all-purpose, bread, cake, whole wheat)
CORNSTARCH
ALL SUGARS
MAPLE SYRUP   PANCAKE SYRUP (corn blend)
MOLASSES (light and blackstrap)
FLAVORINGS AND LIQUEUR EXTRACTS

SWEETENED CONDENSED MILK (canned)
EVAPORATED MILK (canned)

POWDERED DESSERT TOPPING   DRY TAPIOCA

VEGETABLE SHORTENING   GELATINS

ANGEL FOOD CAKE MIX   BROWNIE MIX

NONFAT DRY MILK

CAKE FROSTING MIXES
> Dry pudding mixes vary in sodium content. See page 54 of the SODIUM/CALORIE COUNTER for individual pudding flavors.

"INSTANT" PUDDINGS
BAKING POWDER   BAKING SODA
CAKE MIXES, MUFFIN MIX, PIECRUST MIX, BISCUIT MIX, PANCAKE AND WAFFLE MIX
GRAHAM CRACKER CRUMBS
SELF-RISING FLOUR

SALT—ONE TEASPOON CONTAINS
2,132 MILLIGRAMS OF SODIUM.

SPAGHETTI, NOODLES, RICE, BEANS, SAUCES

RICE (white, brown, and instant) without seasonings

DRY NOODLES

DRY MACARONI

DRY SPAGHETTI

DRIED BEANS

DRIED LENTILS

DRIED PEAS

TOMATO PASTE, PUREE (with no salt added)

PASTA, RICE, and BEANS in dry form are low in sodium content. If salt is added to water during cooking, the green color code does not apply.

PIZZA MIX

DEHYDRATED POTATOES

TOMATO SAUCES

SPAGHETTI SAUCE (MEATLESS OR WITH MEAT)

PACKAGED RICE MIXES: FLAVORED AND SPANISH

ALL DRY GRAVY MIXES

SALAD DRESSINGS, OLIVES, PICKLES, OILS

VINEGARS:
cider, white, and red wine

VEGETABLE OILS:
corn, safflower, cottonseed, sesame, soybean, olive, peanut

See the GREEN-LIGHT recipes on page 71 for low-sodium salad dressings.

See the FLAVOR-MAGIC Chart on pages 68 and 69 for suggested salad seasonings.

MAYONNAISE

MAYONNAISE-TYPE SALAD DRESSING

ALL SALAD DRESSINGS except mayonnaise
(bottled and dry mixes)

IMITATION BACON BITS

CHILI SAUCE KETCHUP BARBECUE SAUCE

OLIVES   PICKLES   PICKLE RELISH

PREPARED MUSTARD

WORCESTERSHIRE SAUCE

HERBS AND SPICES

Allspice, Basil, Bay Leaf, Caraway Seed, Cardamom, Celery Seed, Chervil, Cinnamon, Cloves, Cumin, Dill Seed and Weed, Fennel, Garlic Powder, Ginger, Mace, Marjoram, Dry Mustard, Nutmeg, Onion Powder, Oregano, Paprika, Parsley Flakes, Pepper (Black, Cayenne, and White), Poppy Seed, Poultry Seasoning, Pumpkin Pie Spice, Rosemary, Saffron, Sage, Savory, Sesame Seed, Tarragon, Thyme

SOME CHILI POWDERS CONTAIN SALT.
SOME CURRY POWDERS CONTAIN SALT.

SALT
MONOSODIUM GLUTAMATE (MSG)
CELERY SALT
CHILI POWDER WITH SALT
CURRY POWDER WITH SALT
GARLIC SALT
ONION SALT
SEASONED SALT
GRAVY MIXES (DRY)
IMITATION BACON BITS
SALAD SEASONING
SALAD SEASONING WITH CHEESE

MOST MEAT TENDERIZERS CONTAIN SALT AND/OR MONOSODIUM GLUTAMATE (MSG)

SALT—One teaspoon contains 2,132 milligrams of sodium.

PACKAGED BAKERY: BREADS, ROLLS, CAKES, PIES—COOKIES AND CRACKERS

MATZOS (unsalted)
MELBA TOAST (unsalted)
CRACKERS (unsalted)*

BREADS:
- Raisin
- White enriched
- Cracked wheat
- Rye
- Pumpernickel
- French or Vienna
- Italian
- Whole wheat

BREAD CRUMBS (PLAIN)
CORN FLAKE CRUMBS
ROLLS: BROWN AND SERVE, CLOVERLEAF

Cookies and crackers vary widely among manufacturers, in size, weight, and sodium content.

CHECK THE SODIUM/CALORIE COUNTER at the back of this Supermarket Guide for those cookies with lower sodium content.

NOTE: The sodium listings for *all* cookies and crackers are for *one* piece.

HERB-SEASONED CROUTONS
BREAD STICKS   BREAD STUFFING
ENGLISH MUFFINS
ROLLS: FRANKFURTER, HAMBURGER,
KAISER   CUPCAKES
MINIPIES   DOUGHNUTS
DANISH PASTRY   MINICAKES

---

*Low-sodium breadsticks, cookies, and crackers are available in the dietetic-foods section of your supermarket.

JELLIES, ICE CREAM, CANDY, SYRUPS

ALL JELLIES, JAMS, MARMALADES

HONEY

ICE CREAM

ICE MILK

SHERBET

CHOCOLATE SYRUP (thin and fudge)

GUM DROPS, HARD CANDY, JELLY BEANS

MARSHMALLOWS

PEANUT BUTTER

CANDY

ALL CANDY is listed in the sodium/calorie counter in one-ounce servings.

When selecting candy, check the weight on the package against the one-ounce serving listed in the sodium/calorie counter to determine the number of milligrams of sodium in a serving.

Low-sodium peanut butter is available in the dietetic-foods section of your supermarket.

SNACKS	**BEVERAGES**
UNSALTED NUTS UNSALTED PRETZELS CARAMEL CORN SUNFLOWER SEEDS UNSALTED	TEA COFFEE (ground) COFFEE (dry powder) COCOA (dry powder) WINES BEER COFFEE WHITENER (powdered, nondairy) SOFT DRINKS (Low-calorie soft drinks contain sodium saccharine.)
	COFFEE (flavored, powdered) Hot Cocoa Mix
SALTED NUTS CHEESE SNACK CRACKERS CORN CHIPS POPCORN POTATO CHIPS PRETZELS SOY NUTS	COOKING WINES

SODIUM/CALORIE COUNTER

The foods are listed according to the department in which they are found in the supermarket.

Both the sodium content (in milligrams) and the number of calories are listed in the usual serving size, unless otherwise specified.

FRESH PRODUCE

Fresh Vegetables

Sodium content and calories are based on cooked vegetables, unless otherwise specified.

NAME	AMOUNT	SODIUM (mgs.)	CALORIES
Artichoke (med.)	1 bud	36	10–53*
Asparagus	4 spears	1	12
Beans, green	½ cup	2	17
Beans, lima	½ cup	1	95
Beans, yellow	½ cup	2	14
Beets	½ cup	37	27
Broccoli	½ cup	8	20
Brussels sprouts	½ cup	8	28
Cabbage (raw)	½ cup	7	9
Carrots	½ cup	26	24
Cauliflower	½ cup	6	14
Celery (raw)	½ cup	76	10
Collards	½ cup	18	21
Corn, ear	one ear	trace	70
Cucumber (raw)	½ cup	4	10
Eggplant	½ cup	1	19
Endive (raw)	½ cup	4	5
Garlic (raw)	1 clove	1	4
Green pepper (raw)	½ cup	5	9

*Calories range from 10 calories for freshly harvested artichokes to 53 calories for stored artichokes.

NAME	AMOUNT	SODIUM (mgs.)	CALORIES
Lettuce (raw)	½ cup	3	4
Mushrooms (raw)	½ cup	6	10
Onions	½ cup	8	31
Peas	½ cup	1	57
Potatoes	½ cup	3	59
Spinach	½ cup	45	21
Squash	½ cup	1	15
Sweet potatoes	½ cup	13	146
Swiss chard	½ cup	75	16
Tomatoes (med. raw)	one	trace	27
Turnip	½ cup	27	18
Zucchini	½ cup	1	11

Fresh Fruits

Sodium content and calories are based on raw fruits.

NAME	AMOUNT	SODIUM	CALORIES
Apple (med.)	one	1	61
Apricot (med.)	three	1	55
Avocado	one-half	5	188
Banana (med.)	one	1	101
Blueberries	½ cup	trace	45
Cantaloupe	one-half	33	82
Cherries	½ cup	1	41
Coconut	½ cup	9	139
Cranberries	½ cup	1	22
Grapefruit	one-half	trace	40
Grapefruit juice	½ cup	1	48
Grapes	½ cup	2	35
Honeydew melon	wedge	18	49
Orange (med.)	one	1	71
Orange juice	½ cup	1	66
Peach (med.)	one	1	38
Pear (med.)	one	3	86
Pineapple	½ cup	1	41

Fresh Fruits (continued)

NAME	AMOUNT	SODIUM (mgs.)	CALORIES
Plum (med)	one	1	32
Raspberries (black)	½ cup	trace	49
Raspberries (red)	½ cup	trace	35
Rhubarb	½ cup	1	10
Strawberries	½ cup	trace	28
Tangerine (med.)	one	2	39
Watermelon	1/16th of melon	4	111

Dried Fruits (uncooked):

Apricots	½ cup	17	166
Dates	½ cup	2	311
Figs (med.)	one	1	40
Raisins	½ cup	20	210
Prunes (softened)	½ cup	7	230

Nuts: (shelled, *unsalted*):

Almonds	½ cup	3	425
Brazil	½ cup	trace	458
Cashews	½ cup	11	393
Peanuts	½ cup	4	419
Pecans	½ cup	trace	371
Walnuts, black chopped	½ cup	2	393
Walnuts, English chopped	½ cup	1	391

FRESH MEATS, POULTRY, FISH—PROCESSED MEATS

Sodium content and calories are based on 4 oz. retail cuts, COOKED

FRESH MEATS—LEAN, TRIMMED OF SEPARABLE FAT

NAME	AMOUNT	SODIUM (mgs.)	CALORIES
Beef:			
Chuck rib	4 oz.	57	282
Club steak	4 oz.	82	277
Corned beef brisket	4 oz.	1069	422
Flank	4 oz.	61	222
Ground chuck (21% fat)	4 oz.	67	324
Ground round (10% fat)	4 oz.	76	248
Plate	4 oz.	60	226
Porterhouse steak	4 oz.	84	254
Rib roast	4 oz.	78	273
Round steak	4 oz.	87	214
Rump roast	4 oz.	81	236
Sirloin steak	4 oz.	90	235
T-bone steak	4 oz.	85	253
Lamb:			
Leg	4 oz.	80	211
Loin chops	4 oz.	78	213
Rib chops	4 oz.	76	240
Shoulder	4 oz.	75	233

Fresh Meats (continued)

NAME	AMOUNT	SODIUM (mgs.)	CALORIES
Pork:			
Boston butt	4 oz.	75	277
Ham, canned	4 oz.	1062	219
Ham, fresh	4 oz.	83	246
Ham, light cured (smoked)	4 oz.	1028	212
Loin	4 oz.	82	288
Picnic	4 oz.	58	241
Spareribs	4 oz.	41	499
Veal:			
Breast	4 oz.	52	344
Chuck	4 oz.	56	267
Loin	4 oz.	74	265
Rib	4 oz.	98	305
Organ meats:			
Beef liver	1 slice	156	195
Brains	3 oz.	106	106
Calf liver	1 slice	100	222
Chicken liver	3 small	45	123
Heart	4 oz.	118	213
Kidney (beef)	4 oz.	287	286
Sweetbreads	3 oz.	99	272
Sauerkraut	½ cup	878	21
Lard	1 tablespoon	0	117
Poultry: (without skin)			
Chicken—light meat	4 oz.	74	188
—dark meat	4 oz.	99	199
Turkey—light meat	4 oz.	93	199
—dark meat	4 oz.	112	230

NAME	AMOUNT	SODIUM (mgs.)	CALORIES
Processed Meats:			
Bacon (4 med. slices)	3.2 oz.	306	172
Bacon, Canadian (3 slices)	2 oz.	1611	174
Beef, dried	3 oz.	3657	174
Bologna	1 oz.	305*	95*
Frankfurter (1 wiener)	2 oz.	627	176
Ham, chopped	1 oz.	384*	65*
Ham, loaf	1 oz.	370*	35*
Liverwurst	1¼ oz.	466*	115*
Sausage (3 links)	3 oz.	375	186
Salami	1 oz.	305*	95*
Turkey roll	3½ oz.	685*	120*
Fish: (raw—edible portions)			
Cod	4 oz.	80	89
Haddock	4 oz.	69	90
Halibut	4 oz.	61	114
Lobster (meat only)	4 oz.	153	69
Oysters	4 oz.	83	75
Perch	4 oz.	77	103
Pike	4 oz.	58	106
Salmon (sockeye)	4 oz.	73	136
Scallops	4 oz.	289	92
Shrimp	4 oz.	159	103
Snapper	4 oz.	76	106
Sole	4 oz.	89	90

*Data supplied by manufacturer.

DAIRY AND REFRIGERATED PRODUCTS

NAME	AMOUNT	SODIUM (mgs.)	CALORIES
Butter (unsalted)	1 Tbs.	2	102
Butter, stick (salted)	1 Tbs.	117	102
Butter, whipped (salted)	1 Tbs.	78	68
Margarine, stick (unsalted)	1 Tbs.	1	100
Margarine, stick (salted)	1 Tbs.	140	102
Margarine, whipped, soft tub (salted)	1 Tbs.	93	68
Coffee cream (light)	1 Tbs.	6	29
Cream, half-and-half	1 Tbs.	6	20
Cream, heavy whipping	1 Tbs.	6	52
Cream, sour	1 Tbs.	6	26
Imitation sour cream (nondairy)	1 Tbs.	15	29
Whipped-cream topping (pressurized)	1 Tbs.	4	8
Whole egg	one	69	79

Milk:

Buttermilk, cultured	1 cup	257	99
Skim milk	1 cup	126	86
Low-fat milk 2% fat	1 cup	122	121
Low-fat milk 1% fat	1 cup	123	102
Whole milk 3.3% fat	1 cup	120	150
Whole milk 3.7% fat	1 cup	119	157

NAME	AMOUNT	SODIUM (mgs.)	CALORIES
Chocolate milk (from low-fat, 1% fat)	1 cup	148	158
Chocolate milk (from low-fat, 2% fat)	1 cup	150	179
Chocolate milk (from whole milk)	1 cup	149	208
Eggnog	1 cup	138	342
Yogurt, plain—low-fat	1 cup	159	144
Yogurt, fruit flavored	1 cup	133	231

Cheese:

American (pasteurized)	1 oz.	337	93
Brick	1 oz.	159	105
Blue	1 oz.	396	100
Camembert	1 oz.	239	85
Cheddar	1 oz.	176	114
Colby	1 oz.	171	112
Cottage cheese (creamed)	½ cup	457	117
Cottage cheese (dry)	½ cup	14	96
Cottage cheese (low-fat 1%)	½ cup	459	82
Cottage cheese (low-fat 2%)	½ cup	459	101
Cream cheese	1 oz.	84	99
Edam	1 oz.	274	101
Feta	1 oz.	316	75
Gouda	1 oz.	232	101
Gruyère	1 oz.	95	117

Cheese (continued)

NAME	AMOUNT	SODIUM (mgs.)	CALORIES
Monterey Jack	1 oz.	152	106
Mozzarella (low-moisture, part-skim)	1 oz.	150	79
Neufchatel	1 oz.	113	74
Parmesan (grated)	1 oz.	528	129
Ricotta (part-skim)	½ cup	155	171
Roquefort	1 oz.	513	105
Swiss (pasteurized)	1 oz.	388	95

Refrigerated Products:

Horseradish*	1 Tbs.	14	6
Herring (pickled)	½ cup	**	252
Dill pickles	1 med.	928	15
Refrigerated cookie dough	3 oz.	140	449
Smoked salmon	2 oz.	**	100

*Some manufacturers add salt. Read the ingredient list on the label.
**Prepared in salt brine, no figures on sodium content available.

FROZEN FOODS

NAME	AMOUNT	SODIUM (mgs.)	CALORIES

Frozen Fruits and Fruit Juices:

Blackberries	½ cup	1	46
Blueberries	½ cup	1	46
Cherries, red—sour	½ cup	2	62
Grape juice	½ cup	2	66
Grapefruit juice (unsweetened)	½ cup	1	51
Honeydew melon balls	½ cup	11	72
Lemonade concentrate (diluted)	½ cup	trace	54
Limeade concentrate (diluted)	½ cup	Trace	51
Orange juice (from concentrate)	½ cup	1	61
Raspberries, red	½ cup	2	123
Rhubarb	½ cup	7	85
Strawberries	½ cup	2	139

Frozen Vegetables: (cooked)

Asparagus	½ cup	1	22
Broccoli	½ cup	14	24
Brussels sprouts	½ cup	11	26
Cauliflower	½ cup	9	16
Corn, kernels	½ cup	1	68
Corn, ear	one med.	trace	122
Green beans	½ cup	2	17
Lima beans	½ cup	86	82
Mixed vegetables	½ cup	67	74
Peas	½ cup	92	54

Frozen Vegetables: (cooked) (continued)

NAME	AMOUNT	SODIUM (mgs.)	CALORIES
Potatoes, raw (diced or shredded)	½ cup	6	51
Potatoes, raw (French fried)	10 pcs.	2	110
Spinach, chopped	½ cup	54	24
Squash, winter	½ cup	1	46
Succotash	½ cup	35	75
Yellow beans	½ cup	trace	18

Frozen Vegetables: (with sauces)

Carrots (brown-sugar glaze)	3.3 oz.	500*	80*
Cauliflower with cheese sauce	3.3 oz.	420*	110*
Mixed vegetables with onion sauce	2.6 oz.	340*	110*
Green peas with cream sauce	2.6 oz.	420*	130*

Frozen Fish:

Fried perch	4 oz.	800*	250*
Fried shrimp	3 oz.	480*	170*

Frozen Poultry:

Frozen turkey, butter basted (white meat only)	3.5 oz.	150*	170*
Frozen turkey roll	3.5 oz.	685*	120*

*Data supplied by manufacturer.

NAME	AMOUNT	SODIUM (mgs.)	CALORIES
Frozen Dinners: (one complete dinner)			
Beans and franks	11¼ oz.	1370*	550*
Beef	11½ oz.	1025*	370*
Beef pot pie	8 oz.	1125*	430*
Chicken and noodles	10¼ oz.	1105*	390*
Chicken pot pie	8 oz.	1110*	450*
Chopped sirloin	10 oz.	1105*	460*
Fish and chips	10¼ oz.	695*	450*
Fried chicken	11½ oz.	1615*	570*
Ham	10¼ oz.	1105*	380*
Macaroni and beef	12 oz.	1055*	400*
Spaghetti and meatballs	12½ oz.	1150*	410*
Swiss steak	10 oz.	965*	350*
Turkey	11½ oz.	1060*	360*
Veal parmigiana	12¼ oz.	1110*	520*
Egg substitutes	¼ cup	130–150*	70–80*
Coffee whitener (nondairy)	1 Tbs.	12	20
Dessert topping (nondairy), pressurized	1 Tbs.	2	11
Dessert topping (nondairy), semisolid	1 Tbs.	1	13
Frozen Bakery:			
Blueberry muffin	one	132*	120*
Corn muffin	one	281*	130*
Parkerhouse roll	one	130*	75*
Poppy seed roll	one	98*	55*
Sesame seed roll	one	98*	55*
Doughnut, glazed	one	76*	150*
Doughnut, jelly	one	73*	180*

Frozen Bakery (continued)

NAME	AMOUNT	SODIUM (mgs.)	CALORIES
Frozen pizza (5" indiv.)	one	472	178
Waffle (10 in 12 oz. package)	one	219	86
Apple pie	1/6 pie	195	231
Cherry pie	1/6 pie	222	282
Coconut cream pie	1/6 pie	252	249
Banana cake	1/8 cake	154*	175*
Chocolate brownie	1/8 cake	108*	200*
Devil's food cake	1/6 cake	357	323

---

*Data supplied by manufacturer.

CEREALS AND TOASTER PASTRIES

The sodium contents and calories for some hot cereals have been taken directly from the nutrition information on the package. Data on other cereals have been supplied by manufacturers.

NAME	AMOUNT	SODIUM (mgs.)	CALORIES
Hot Cereals: (uncooked, without added milk)			
Cream of Rice	¾ cup	10	120
Cream of Wheat Regular	1 oz.	10	100
Cream of Wheat Instant	1 oz.	10	100
Cream of Wheat Quick	1 oz.	130	100
Cream of Wheat Mix-N-Eat	1 oz.	265	100
Cream of Wheat Mix-N-Eat Maple Flavor	1¼ oz.	300	130
Malt-O-Meal Quick	1 oz.	2	100
Maypo 30-second	1 oz.	5	110
Quaker Hot and Creamy	1 oz.	1	101
Quaker Whole Wheat	1 oz.	1	100
Quaker Oats, Quick or Old Fashioned	1 oz.	1	109
Quaker Oatmeal, Instant	1 packet	252	105
Quaker Oatmeal, Instant Apples and Cinnamon	1 packet	181	134

Hot Cereals: (uncooked, without added milk) (continued)

NAME	AMOUNT	SODIUM (mgs.)	CALORIES
Quaker Oatmeal, Instant Maple and Brown Sugar	1 packet	228	163
Quaker Oatmeal, Instant Raisins and Spice	1 packet	227	159
Quaker Instant Grits	1 packet	379	79
Quaker Instant Grits with Imitation Bacon Bits	1 packet	544	101
Quaker Instant Grits with Imitation Ham Bits	1 packet	658	99
Ralston Regular	1 oz.	5	110
Wheatena	1 oz.	5	110

Ready-to-Eat Cereals:

Since sodium content on ready-to-eat cereals varies among manufacturers, the figures for sodium and calories have been taken from the United States Department of Agriculture Handbook #456.

Bran Cereal Products:

Bran flakes (40%)	1 cup	207	106
Bran flakes with raisins	1 cup	212	144
Bran with wheat germ	2 Tbs.	46	22
Bran with malt extract	2 Tbs.	62	18

NAME	AMOUNT	SODIUM (mgs.)	CALORIES
Corn Cereal Products:			
Corn flakes	1 cup	251	97
Sugar-coated corn flakes	1 cup	267	154
Puffed corn	1 cup	233	80
Cocoa-flavored corn	1 cup	255	117
Fruit-flavored corn	1 cup	228	119
Oat Cereal Products:			
Shredded oats with sugar	1 cup	275	171
Puffed oats with sugar	1 cup	317	99
Puffed oats with corn	1 cup	206	139
Rice Cereal Products:			
Puffed rice	1 cup	trace	60
Puffed rice with cocoa	1 cup	148	140
Oven-popped rice with sugar	1 cup	283	117
Shredded rice with sugar	1 cup	229	98
Wheat Cereal Products:			
Wheat, puffed (plain)	1 cup	1	54
Wheat, puffed with sugar	1 cup	56	132
Wheat and malted barley (flakes)	1 cup	226	157

Wheat Cereal Products (continued)

NAME	AMOUNT	SODIUM (mgs.)	CALORIES
Wheat and malted barley (granules)	½ cup	407	215
Wheat flakes with sugar	1 cup	310	106
Wheat germ (plain)	1 Tbs.	trace	23
Shredded wheat	1 biscuit	1	89
Shredded wheat, spoon size (50 small)	1 cup	2	177
"Natural" cereals	1 oz.	50*	130*
Breakfast bars (choc. chip)	1 bar	163*	200*
Cornmeal (enriched)	1 cup	1	502
Cornmeal (self-rising)	1 cup	1849	465
Toaster Pastries:			
Plain: (one pastry)			
Blueberry	one	251*	210*
Brown sugar-cinnamon	one	230*	210*
Strawberry	one	235*	210*
Raspberry	one	227*	210*
Frosted: (one pastry)			
Blueberry	one	226*	210*
Brown sugar-cinnamon	one	225*	210*
Strawberry	one	226*	210*
Raspberry	one	263*	210*

*Data supplied by manufacturer.

CANNED FOODS

NAME	AMOUNT	SODIUM (mgs.)	CALORIES

Fruits and Fruit Juices:

NAME	AMOUNT	SODIUM	CALORIES
Apple juice	½ cup	1	59
Apple sauce	½ cup	3	50
Apricots (heavy syrup)	½ cup	2	111
Apricot nectar	½ cup	trace	72
Blackberries	½ cup	2	117
Cherries (heavy syrup)	½ cup	2	104
Cherries (sour)	½ cup	3	53
Cranberry juice	½ cup	2	82
Cranberry sauce	½ cup	2	202
Figs	½ cup	3	109
Fruit cocktail	½ cup	7	97
Grape drink	½ cup	2	68
Grape juice	½ cup	3	84
Grapefruit sections	½ cup	2	89
Grapefruit juice	½ cup	1	52
Orange juice	½ cup	1	60
Peaches (heavy syrup)	½ cup	3	100
Pears (heavy syrup)	½ cup	2	97
Pineapple (in its own juice)	½ cup	1	48
Pineapple (heavy syrup)	½ cup	2	117
Pineapple juice	½ cup	2	69
Plums (heavy syrup)	½ cup	2	107
Prune juice	½ cup	3	99
Pumpkin	½ cup	3	40

Canned Foods (continued)

NAME	AMOUNT	SODIUM (mgs.)	CALORIES
Canned Vegetables (drained solids) and Vegetable Juices:			
Asparagus	½ cup	278	26
Beans, green	½ cup	160	16
Beans, lima	½ cup	202	82
Beans, yellow	½ cup	282	23
Beets (sliced)	½ cup	201	32
Carrots	½ cup	183	24
Corn, whole kernel	½ cup	248	87
Corn, cream style	½ cup	302	105
Mushrooms	½ cup	404	18
Peas	½ cup	202	75
Sauerkraut	½ cup	878	21
Spinach	½ cup	242	25
Sweet potatoes	½ cup	48	108
Tomatoes (solids and liquids)	½ cup	157	26
Tomato juice	½ cup	243	23
Vegetable juice cocktail	½ cup	242	21
Soups: (canned, prepared with equal amounts of water)			
Beef noodle	1 cup	917	67
Chicken noodle	1 cup	979	62
Chicken rice	1 cup	917	48
Cream of chicken	1 cup	970	94
Manhattan clam chowder	1 cup	938	81
Minestrone	1 cup	995	105
Onion	1 cup	1051	65
Pea	1 cup	899	130

NAME	AMOUNT	SODIUM (mgs.)	CALORIES
Tomato	1 cup	970	88
Turkey noodle	1 cup	998	79
Vegetarian vegetable	1 cup	838	78
Vegetable beef	1 cup	1046	78

Soups: (Canned, prepared with equal amounts of milk)

Cream of celery	1 cup	1039	169
Cream of chicken	1 cup	1054	179
Cream of mushroom	1 cup	1039	216
Tomato	1 cup	1055	173
Pea	1 cup	983	213

Soups: dehydrated (prepared as directed on package)

Beef noodle	1 cup	420	67
Bouillon cube	one	960	5
Chicken noodle	1 cup	578	53
Onion	1 cup	689	36
Tomato-vegetable	1 cup	1025	65

Canned Fish:

Crabmeat	¼ cup	338	34
Salmon (pink)	½ cup	439	160
Salmon (red, sockeye)	½ cup	592	194
Sardines (in oil)	3¾ oz. can	541	330
Shrimp	20 small	168	152
Tuna fish (water pack)	3½ oz. can	866	126

Canned Foods (continued)

NAME	AMOUNT	SODIUM (mgs.)	CALORIES

Ready-to-Serve Main Dishes:

Beans and franks	1 cup	1374	367
Baked beans in tomato sauce	1 cup	862	306
Chili con carne	1 cup	1354	339
Macaroni and cheese	1 cup	730	228
Pork and beans	1 cup	1181	311
Processed canned meats:			
Pork, chopped (spiced/unspiced)	2 oz.	700	167
Pork sausage	2 patties	740	299
Vienna sausage	2 oz.	590	127
Spaghetti and meatballs	1 cup	1220	258
Spaghetti, tomato sauce with cheese	1 cup	955	190
Vegetable and beef stew	1 cup	1007	194

Chinese Foods:

Chop suey with meat	8 oz.	1250	141
Chow mein with chicken	8 oz.	658	86
Soy sauce	1 Tbs.	1319	12

The sodium and calorie contents of Tomato Paste, Tomato Puree, and Spaghetti Sauces are listed on page 57.

CAKE AND PIE MIXES, DESSERTS, BAKING AIDS

The serving size of some products in this department is figured for a whole recipe, rather than a usual serving. NOTE THE SERVING SIZE when checking sodium content on a particular food.

NAME	AMOUNT	SODIUM (mgs.)	CALORIES
Cake flour (enriched)*	1 cup	2	430
Bread flour (enriched)*	1 cup	2	420
All-purpose flour (enriched)	1 cup	3	455
Self-rising flour** (enriched)*	1 cup	1241	405
Whole wheat flour	1 cup	4	400
Biscuit mix (dry) (enriched flour)	½ cup	780	255
Graham cracker crumbs for piecrusts	1 cup	529	432
Piecrust mix	10 oz. package	1968	1482
Sugars:			
Brown	1 cup	66	821
Confectioners	1 cup	1	462
White granulated	1 cup	2	770

*"Enriched" means that vitamins have been added.
**"Self-rising" means that sodium-containing leavening ingredients have been added.

Cake and Pie Mixes, Desserts, Baking Aids (continued)

NAME	AMOUNT	SODIUM (mgs.)	CALORIES
Syrups:			
Maple syrup	1 Tbs.	2	50
Molasses (light)	1 Tbs.	3	50
Molasses (blackstrap)	1 Tbs.	19	43
Pancake syrup (corn blend)	1 Tbs.	14	59
Cakes: (made from baking mix) one piece			
Angel food	1/12 of whole	77	137
Brownies	one brownie	33	86
Chocolate cake	1/12 of whole	283	308
Coffee cake	1/6 of whole	310	232
Devil's food	1/12 of whole	241	312
Honey spice	1/12 of whole	252	363
White	1/12 of whole	216	333
Yellow	1/12 of whole	209	310
Corn muffin mix	one muffin	192	130
Cornbread mix	one piece	263	178
Pancake and waffle mix (dry)	1/2 cup	1053	262

NAME	AMOUNT	SODIUM (mgs.)	CALORIES
Frosting:			
Chocolate fudge	¼ cup	121	293
Creamy fudge	¼ cup	142	208
Powdered dessert topping (nondairy)	1 Tbs.	2	8

Flavorings and Liqueur Extracts contain flavor essence and alcohol only. They contain a trace of sodium and a few calories.

Milks:

Milk, condensed, sweetened	¼ cup	98	246
Milk, evaporated, skim	¼ cup	74	50
Milk, evaporated, whole	¼ cup	67	85
Nonfat dry milk, reconstituted	1 Tbs.	23*	15*
	8 fl. oz.	124*	80*

Baking Aids:

Baking soda	1 tsp.	1123	0
Baking powder	1 tsp.	329	4
Chocolate (baking, bitter)	1 oz.	1	143
Chocolate (semi-sweet morsels)	1 oz.	1	144
Cornstarch	1 tsp.	trace	29
Coconut (shredded)	½ cup	9	139
Salt	1 tsp.	2132	0
Tapioca (dry)	1 Tbs.	trace	30
Vegetable shortening (solid)	1 Tbs.	1	111

*Data supplied by manufacturer.

Cake and Pie Mixes, Desserts, Baking Aids (continued)

NAME	AMOUNT	SODIUM (mgs.)	CALORIES

Gelatins: (prepared as directed on package)

Gelatin, unflavored dry	1 Tbs.	11	34
Gelatin, flavored: apricot, blackberry, black cherry, mixed fruit, orange, peach, raspberry, strawberry, and strawberry-banana			
	½ cup	55*	80*
Black raspberry and concord grape	½ cup	40*	80*
Cherry and wild raspberry	½ cup	80*	80*
Wild cherry	½ cup	95*	80*

Puddings: (prepared as directed on package)

Tapioca pudding, chocolate	½ cup	165*	160*
Tapioca pudding, vanilla	½ cup	175*	160*
Rice pudding	½ cup	160*	170*
Pudding and pie filling: (regular)			
Butterscotch	½ cup	245*	170*
Chocolate	½ cup	195*	170*
Vanilla	½ cup	200*	160*
Banana cream	⅙ of 8" pie	165*	110*
Coconut cream	⅙ of 9" pie	135*	110*
Lemon	⅙ of 9" pie	95*	180*

*Data supplied by manufacturer.

NAME	AMOUNT	SODIUM (mgs.)	CALORIES
Pudding and pie filling: (instant)			
Banana cream	½ cup	405*	180*
Butterscotch	½ cup	445*	170*
Chocolate	½ cup	470*	190*
Coconut cream	½ cup	310*	180*
Lemon	½ cup	360*	180*
Pistachio	½ cup	400*	180*
Vanilla	½ cup	400*	180*

*Data supplied by manufacturer.

SPAGHETTI, NOODLES, RICE, BEANS, SAUCES

NAME	AMOUNT	SODIUM (mgs.)	CALORIES
Gravy Mixes: (prepared as directed on package)			
Au jus gravy mix	¼ cup	228*	8*
Brown gravy mix	¼ cup	259*	15*
Chicken gravy mix	¼ cup	428*	22*
Mushroom gravy mix	¼ cup	292*	15*
Onion gravy mix	¼ cup	238*	21*
Turkey gravy mix	¼ cup	332*	23*
Beans: (dried)			
Barley, pearled	½ cup	3	348
Gr. northern or navy	½ cup	7	306
Dried chickpeas	½ cup	26	360
Dried peas	½ cup	35	340
Dried kidney beans	½ cup	10	317
Dried lentils	½ cup	29	323
Dried lima beans	½ cup	4	310
Dried pinto beans	½ cup	10	332
Noodles, pasta: (cooked without salt)			
Macaroni	½ cup	trace	96
Noodles, egg	½ cup	2	100
Spaghetti, plain	½ cup	trace	78
Rice: (cooked, prepared as directed on package, with added salt)			
Brown	½ cup	225	116
Flavored rice mix	½ cup	460–700*	120*
Instant	½ cup	225	90
Spanish rice mix	½ cup	650*	100*
White long grain	½ cup	384	112

*Data supplied by manufacturer.

NAME	AMOUNT	SODIUM (mgs.)	CALORIES

Bottled and canned sauces:

Spaghetti sauce (meatless)	4 oz.	670*	70*
Spaghetti sauce (with meat)	4 oz.	775*	100*
Tomato paste	2 oz.	23*	50*
Tomato puree	4 oz.	23*	50*
Tomato sauce	4 oz.	500*	40*

Potatoes: (prepared as directed on package)

Dehydrated mashed flakes	½ cup	243	98
Dehydrated mashed granules	½ cup	246	83
Dehydrated potatoes, au gratin	½ cup	555*	90*
Dehydrated potatoes, creamed	½ cup	320*	90*

> Look for dried potato products that DO NOT LIST SALT AS AN INGREDIENT, and prepare potatoes without adding salt.

Pizza mixes:

Cheese pizza mix	3¾ oz.	735*	220*
Pepperoni pizza mix	4¼ oz.	870*	270*
Sausage pizza mix	4¼ oz.	930*	280*

---

*Data supplied by manufacturer.

SALAD DRESSINGS, OLIVES, PICKLES, OILS

NAME	AMOUNT	SODIUM (mgs.)	CALORIES
Cooking Oils:			
Vegetable Oils	1 Tbs.	0	120
Olives and Pickles:			
Green olives (large)	five	463	23
Ripe olives (mammoth)	five	228	36
Pickles, bread and butter	6 slices	337	37
Pickles, dill (med.)	one	928	7
Pickle relish	1 Tbs.	107	21
All vinegars	1 Tbs.	trace	2
Bacon bits, imitation	1 tsp.	229*	8*
Salad Dressings: (bottled)			
Blue, roquefort	1 Tbs.	164	76
French	1 Tbs.	219	66
Italian	1 Tbs.	314	83
Thousand island	1 Tbs.	112	80
Mayonnaise	1 Tbs.	84	101
Mayonnaise-type dressing	1 Tbs.	88	65
Salad Dressings: (dry mix)			
French creamy	1 Tbs.	125	70*
Italian	1 Tbs.	105	60*
Condiments:			
Barbecue sauce	1 Tbs.	127	14
Chili sauce	1 Tbs.	201	16
Mustard, prepared	1 Tbs.	189	12
Tomato ketchup	1 Tbs.	156	16
Worcestershire sauce	1 Tbs.	149	12

*Data supplied by manufacturer.

HERBS AND SPICES

NAME	AMOUNT	SODIUM (mgs.)	CALORIES
Allspice	1 tsp.	1	5
Bacon bits, imitation	1 tsp.	229*	8*
Basil	1 tsp.	trace	4
Bay leaf	1 tsp.	trace	2
Caraway seed	1 tsp.	trace	7
Cardamom	1 tsp.	trace	6
Celery salt	1 tsp.	1275*	8*
Celery seed	1 tsp.	3	8
Chervil	1 tsp.	trace	1
Chili powder with salt	1 tsp.	46*	8*
Cinnamon	1 tsp.	1	6
Cloves (ground)	1 tsp.	5	7
Cumin	1 tsp.	4	8
Curry powder with no salt added	1 tsp.	1	6
Curry powder with salt added	1 tsp.	67*	6*
Dill seed	1 tsp.	trace	6
Dill weed	1 tsp.	2	3
Fennel	1 tsp.	2	7
Garlic powder	1 tsp.	1	9
Garlic salt	1 tsp.	1242*	9*
Ginger	1 tsp.	1	6
Mace	1 tsp.	1	8
Marjoram	1 tsp.	trace	2
MSG (monosodium glutamate)	1 tsp.	500	2
Mustard, dry	1 tsp.	trace	15

*Data supplied by manufacturer.

HERBS AND SPICES (continued)

NAME	AMOUNT	SODIUM (mgs.)	CALORIES
Nutmeg	1 tsp.	trace	12
Onion powder	1 tsp.	1	7
Onion salt	1 tsp.	1100*	7*
Oregano	1 tsp.	trace	5
Paprika	1 tsp.	1	6
Parsley (dry)	1 tsp.	1	1
Pepper:			
Black	1 tsp.	1	5
Cayenne	1 tsp.	1	6
White	1 tsp.	2	7
Poppy seeds	1 tsp.	1	15
Poultry seasoning	1 tsp.	trace	5
Pumpkin pie spice	1 tsp.	1	6
Rosemary	1 tsp.	1	4
Saffron	1 tsp.	trace	2
Sage	1 tsp.	trace	2
Salad seasoning	1 tsp.	1151*	4*
Salad seasoning with cheese	1 tsp.	786*	10*
Salt	1 tsp.	2132	0
Savory	1 tsp.	trace	4
Seasoned salt	1 tsp.	1813*	19*
Sesame seeds	1 tsp.	1	16
Tarragon	1 tsp.	1	5
Thyme	1 tsp.	1	4

If mixed herb or spice products are not listed above, READ THE LABEL TO DETERMINE IF SALT OR SODIUM is an ingredient.

---

*Data supplied by manufacturer.

PACKAGED BAKERY: BREAD, ROLLS, CAKES AND PIES—COOKIES AND CRACKERS

NAME	AMOUNT	SODIUM (mgs.)	CALORIES
Breads:			
Cracked wheat	1 slice	132	66
French or Vienna	1 slice	145	73
Italian	1 slice	176	83
Pumpernickel	1 slice	182	79
Raisin	1 slice	91	66
Rye	1 slice	139	61
White enriched	1 slice	127	68
Whole wheat	1 slice	132	61
Rolls:			
Brown and serve	1 roll	136	84
English muffin	one	250*	130*
Frankfurter	1 roll	202	119
Hamburger	1 roll	202	119
Kaiser	1 roll	313	156
Bread Products:			
Bread crumbs (plain)	2 Tbs.	91	49
Bread sticks	one	548	106
Bread stuffing (dry)	¼ cup	233	65
Corn flake crumbs	2 Tbs.	107	41
Herb-seasoned croutons	2 Tbs.	397*	50*
Cakes, Pies, Doughnuts, Danishes:			
Cupcakes (chocolate)	one	250*	160*
Cakes, filled, miniature	one	190*	140*
Danish pastry,	one	238	274
Doughnut, plain	1½ oz.	210	164
Pies: (individual)			
Apple	4½ oz.	415*	400*
Cherry	4½ oz.	412*	420*

*Data supplied by manufacturer.

PACKAGED BAKERY: BREAD, ROLLS, CAKES AND PIES—COOKIES AND CRACKERS

NAME	AMOUNT	SODIUM (mgs.)	CALORIES
Cookies:			
Brownie	one	49	103
Butter wafer	one	21	23
Chocolate chip	one	42	50
Coconut bar	one	13	45
Fig bar	one	35	50
Ginger snap	one	40	29
Graham cracker, chocolate covered	one	53	62
Lady finger	one	8	40
Macaroon	one	7	91
Marshmallow	one	38	73
Molasses	one	125	137
Oatmeal raisin	one	21	59
Sandwich, chocolate or vanilla	one	48	50
Sugar wafer	one	5	46
Vanilla wafer	one	10	19
Crackers:			
Butter cracker	one	36	15
Cheese cracker	one	33	15
Graham cracker (plain)	one	95	55
Graham cracker (sugar honey)	one	72	58
Rye wafer (whole grain)	one	57	22
Saltine	one	31	12
Soda cracker	one	55	22
Zwieback	one	18	30

JELLIES, ICE CREAM, SYRUPS, CANDY

NAME	AMOUNT	SODIUM (mgs.)	CALORIES
Jellies:			
Jellies	1 Tbs.	3	49
Apple butter	1 Tbs.	trace	33
Honey	1 Tbs.	1	64
Jams and preserves	1 Tbs.	1	54
Orange marmalade	1 Tbs.	3	51
Peanut butter	1 Tbs.	97	94
Ice Cream Products:			
Ice cream (16% fat)	½ cup	25	165
Ice cream (10% fat)	½ cup	42	129
Ice milk	½ cup	45	100
Orange sherbet	½ cup	10	130
Syrups:			
Chocolate syrup (thin)	2 Tbs.	20	92
Chocolate syrup (fudge)	2 Tbs.	33	124
Candy:			
Butterscotch	1 oz.	19	113
Candy corn	1 oz.	60	103
Caramel	1 oz.	64	113
Chocolate caramel	1 oz.	58	121
Chocolate (milk with almonds)	1 oz.	23	151
Chocolate-covered raisins	1 oz.	18	120
Cream mints	1 oz.	52	116
Gum drops	1 oz.	10	98
Hard candy	1 oz.	9	109
Jelly beans	1 oz.	3	104
Marshmallow	one	3	23

SNACKS AND BEVERAGES

NAME	AMOUNT	SODIUM (mgs.)	CALORIES
Caramel corn	1 cup	trace	134
Cheese snack crackers	ten	325	150
Cheese stick crackers	ten	95	44
Corn chips	1 oz.	220*	170*
Popcorn	1 cup	175	41
Potato chips	10 chips	68–200**	114*
Pretzels (3-ring)	ten	504	117
Pretzels (thin-type)	ten	1008	234

Nuts:

NAME	AMOUNT	SODIUM	CALORIES
Almonds (unsalted)	9–10 nuts	trace	60
Cashews (unsalted)	7 nuts	2	80
Peanuts (unsalted)	10 nuts	1	105
Peanuts (salted) Spanish	1 oz.	119	166
Pecans (unsalted)	10 halves	trace	62
Soy nuts	1 oz.	220*	130*
Sunflower seeds (unsalted)	1 oz.	6	102

Beverages:

NAME	AMOUNT	SODIUM	CALORIES
Club soda	8 oz.	60	0*
Coca-Cola	8 oz.	3	104
Ginger ale	8 oz.	18	80
Pepsi-Cola	8 oz.	35	106
Cocoa, dry powder	1 Tbs.	trace	14
Cocoa mix, hot	1 oz.	145*	120*
Coffee, dry powder	1 Tbs.	2	3
Coffee, flavored, powder (prepared)	6 oz.	40–140*	50–60*

NAME	AMOUNT	SODIUM (mgs.)	CALORIES
Coffee, ground (prepared)	5 oz.	1	2
Coffee whitener (powdered non-dairy)	1 tsp.	4	11
Tea (prepared)	8 oz.	trace	2
Wine, cooking	2 oz.	372*	19*
Wine, dessert	3½ oz.	4	141
Wine, table	3½ oz.	5	87
Beer	8 oz.	8	114

*Data supplied by manufacturer.
**Amount varies among manufacturers.

PART IV

COLOR-CODED COOKING GUIDE

INTRODUCTION

USE THE COLOR CODE TO COMPARE AND BEWARE

COMPARE THE LOW-SODIUM FOODS that you can cook in your own kitchen to the high-sodium processed foods you find in the supermarket.

BEWARE THE HIGH-SODIUM COMMERCIALLY PREPARED PRODUCTS.

This section will make you keenly aware of the HIGH SODIUM content of "convenience" foods—packaged, canned, and frozen. It will show you how to cook the foods low in sodium content in your own kitchen.

The "convenience" foods that are commercially prepared are higher in sodium than foods we cook in our own kitchens, because salt (sodium chloride) is used in the food processing.

The U.S. Senate Select Committee on Nutrition and Human Needs tells us why:

Salt is added to processed food principally as a flavoring agent rather than as a preservative. In some instances it is the primary flavoring agent and may be used to mask other, less appealing flavors.

TO HELP YOURSELF PREPARE LOW-SODIUM FOODS, USE THE FLAVOR-MAGIC CHART on the following two pages for creative seasonings without salt.

AVOID "CONVENIENCE" FOODS—USE THE CONVENIENT RECIPES beginning on page 75* to prepare tasty low-sodium foods at home.

---

*The sodium contents and calories for the recipes in this section were calculated by the HVH-CWRU Nutrient Data Base at Case Western Reserve University.

FLAVOR-MAGIC CHART

Match each flavor with the food listed below. Read across each row to find "Flavor Magic" for each food.

Flavors	Lemon Juice	Red Wine	White Wine	Sherry Wine	Garlic Fresh/ Powder	Chives/ Onion Powder
Beef		●		●	●	●
Chicken	●	●	●	●	●	●
Lamb		●			●	●
Pork			●	●		●
Veal	●		●	●	●	●
Fish, Shellfish	●		●		●	●
Salad Dressings	●	●	●		●	●
Vegetables: Asparagus	●		●			●
Beets						
Broccoli	●				●	●
Carrots	●			●		
Eggplant					●	●
Green Beans	●				●	●
Lima Beans						●
Mushrooms	●	●	●		●	●
Potatoes						●
Spinach	●				●	●
Squash				●		
Sweet Potatoes				●		
Tomatoes		●	●		●	●
Zucchini	●				●	●

Jams Jellies	Bay Leaf	Basil	Dill	Ginger	Thyme	Dry Mustard
	●	●	●		●	●
Apricot			●	●	●	●
Pineapple	●	●	●	●		
Plum		●	●	●		●
Currant		●	●		●	
	●	●	●	●	●	●
	●	●	●			●
Orange/		●				●
	●		●	●	●	●
		●				●
Currant	●	●	●	●	●	
	●	●	●			
	●	●	●		●	
	●	●				●
	●	●	●		●	
		●	●			●
	●	●				
Pineapple			●	●		
Orange/ Apricot				●		
	●	●	●		●	●
	●	●	●			

COMPARE AND BEWARE

YOU CAN CHOOSE HOW MUCH SODIUM YOU EAT!

The chart below shows you how to reduce the sodium content in a single food by hundreds—and sometimes thousands—of milligrams.

COMPARE	BEWARE
FRESH FOODS	**COMMERCIALLY PREPARED PRODUCTS**
One Whole Cucumber 18 mgs.	One Whole Dill Pickle (medium) 928 mgs.
Fresh Lean Beef 4 oz—57 mgs.	Corned Beef 4 oz.—1069 mgs.
	Dried Beef 3 oz.—3657 mgs.
Fresh Pork (Boston butt) 4 oz.—75 mgs.	Cured Ham 4 oz.—1028 mgs.
	Canadian Bacon 3 slices—1611 mgs.
	Frankfurters (2 weiners) 4 oz.—1254 mgs.
Raw Cabbage (shredded) ½ cup—7 mgs.	Canned Sauerkraut ½ cup—878 mgs.
Fresh Salmon 4 oz.—73 mgs.	Canned Salmon (Pink) 4 oz.—439 mgs.
Fresh Tomatoes 2 raw (medium)—trace of sodium	Canned Tomatoes ½ cup—157 mgs.

SALAD DRESSINGS

COMPARE

GREEN-LIGHT SALAD DRESSINGS:
(Recipes below)

Italian
Trace of Sodium

French
Trace of Sodium

BEWARE

COMMERCIAL SALAD DRESSINGS:

Italian (bottled)
1 Tbs.—314 mgs.
Italian (dry mix)**
1 Tbs.—105 mgs.*
French (bottled)
1 Tbs.—219 mgs.
French (dry mix)**
1 Tbs.—125 mgs.*

BASIC SALAD DRESSING (1 cup)
¼ cup red wine vinegar
¾ cup vegetable oil
1 tsp. dry mustard
½ tsp. fresh ground pepper

FRENCH DRESSING	ITALIAN DRESSING
Basic dressing plus:	Basic dressing plus:
½ tsp. onion powder	1 clove garlic (crushed)
½ tsp. basil	1 tsp. oregano
½ tsp. parsley flakes	

Combine all ingredients in a glass jar. Shake well before using.

Add your favorite herbs to Basic Salad Dressing for a variety of flavors.

---

*Data supplied by manufacturer.
**Prepared as directed on package.

FLAVOR-IT WITHOUT SALT

Tomato products have become a necessity to the American way of eating. Most people don't realize that, with each tablespoon of ketchup on their hamburger, they add 156 mgs. of sodium.

It's difficult to avoid eating a food that does not contain some commercially prepared tomato product: ketchup, chili sauce, canned tomatoes, tomato sauce, tomato juice, tomato soup, baked beans, spaghetti, chili, taco filling, and pizza. All of these are high in sodium content.

It will be easy to give up these high sodium tomato products after you've tried our exclusive low sodium Flavor-It sauce. You'll save money, too, by not buying expensive commercial low-sodium ketchup or chili sauce.

FLAVOR-IT SAUCE can be made with fresh tomatoes or tomato paste. Make a batch to keep in the refrigerator or freezer. Use either recipe (pages 75 and 76).

The following recipes show you how to do it yourself with Flavor-It sauce. These recipes are LOW IN CALORIES as well as LOW IN SODIUM.

Minestrone Soup	Baked Beans
Swiss Steak	Rump Roast
Ground Steak Belmont	Herbed Meat Loaf
Beef Stew	Paprika Pork Chops
Taco Filling	Leg-O-Lamb
Spaghetti and Meatballs	Chicken Mexican
Spanish Rice	Fresh Fish Broil

NOTE: The calorie and sodium values on these recipes are based on the use of precise and accurate measurements. However, when an ingredient is termed "medium" or "large" in a recipe, the Nutrient Data Base made an approximate value. The size of a "medium" ingredient you use at home may differ from the one analyzed by the Data Base, so sodium and calorie values may vary slightly.

COMPARE	**BEWARE**
LOW-SODIUM* DO-IT-YOURSELF RECIPES:	HIGH-SODIUM* COMMERCIALLY PREPARED FOOD:
Flavor-It Sauce (made with fresh tomatoes) 1 Tbs.—1.4 mgs.	Ketchup 1 Tbs. 156 mgs. Chili Sauce 1 Tbs.—201 mgs.
Flavor-It Sauce (made with tomato paste) 1 Tbs.—4 mgs. Recipe on page 75	Tomato Sauce (Canned) 4 oz.—500 mgs. Tomatoes (Canned) ½ cup—157 mgs.
Flavor-It Minestrone Soup One serving—24 mgs. Recipe on page 77	Minestrone Soup (Canned) One serving—995 mgs.
Flavor-It Swiss Steak One serving—59 mgs. Recipe on page 78	Swiss Steak (Frozen) One complete dinner (10 oz.)—965 mgs.
Flavor-It Taco Filling One serving—49 mgs. Recipe on page 81	Packaged Taco Filling** One serving—2230 mgs.

*Sodium content is in milligrams.   **Data supplied by manufacturer.

COMPARE	BEWARE
LOW-SODIUM DO-IT-YOURSELF RECIPES:	HIGH-SODIUM COMMERCIALLY PREPARED FOOD:
Flavor-It Spanish Rice One serving— 17 mgs. Recipe on page 83	Dry Mix Spanish Rice One serving— 650 mgs.
Flavor-It Ground Steak Belmont One serving— 53 mgs. Recipe on page 79	Dry Mix Hamburger Seasoning* (with meat) One serving— 506 mgs.
Flavor-It Baked Beans One serving— 36 mgs. Recipe on page 84	Baked Beans (canned) One serving— 862 mgs.
Flavor-It Beef Stew One serving— 97 mgs. Recipe on page 80	Beef Stew (canned) One serving— 1007 mgs.
Flavor-It Spaghetti and Meatballs One serving— 68 mgs. Recipe on page 82	Spaghetti and Meatballs (canned) One serving— 1220 mgs.

*Data supplied by manufacturer.

FLAVOR-IT RECIPES

FLAVOR-IT SAUCE
WITH TOMATO PASTE

FLAVOR-IT SAUCE
(1¾ cups)

1 can tomato paste (6 oz.)	1 clove garlic (crushed)
1¼ cups water	¼ cup light brown sugar
1 medium onion (sliced)	2 Tbs. sugar
¼ tsp. thyme	2 Tbs. white vinegar
1 bay leaf	1 tsp. cornstarch
¼ tsp. marjoram	dash of cayenne pepper, celery seed, dry mustard

Combine all ingredients in saucepan. Cook for 10 minutes over low heat, stirring constantly. Remove from heat. Place in blender. Blend for 1 minute.

For convenience, prepare a double recipe of FLAVOR-IT SAUCE. You may store it in a jar in the refrigerator, or in a plastic container in the freezer.

One tablespoon of Flavor-It Sauce contains 4 mgs. of sodium and 18 calories.
One-half cup of Flavor-It Sauce contains 32 mgs. of sodium.

The sodium content of the following recipes using Flavor-It Sauce is based on this recipe with tomato paste.

FLAVOR-IT SAUCE WITH FRESH TOMATOES

FLAVOR-IT SAUCE
(2 cups)

- 4 large tomatoes (fresh)
- 1 medium onion (sliced)
- ¼ tsp. thyme
- 1 bay leaf
- ¼ tsp. marjoram
- 1 clove garlic (crushed)
- ¼ cup light brown sugar
- 2 Tbs. sugar
- 2 Tbs. white vinegar
- 1 tsp. cornstarch

dash of cayenne pepper,
celery seed, dry mustard

Slice tomatoes and place in saucepan. Add onion, thyme, bay leaf, marjoram, and garlic. Cover pan and simmer until tomatoes are soft. Remove from heat. Place in blender. Blend one minute; return mixture to saucepan. Add remaining ingredients and simmer, uncovered, for another 10 minutes, stirring occasionally.

When tomatoes are in season, prepare a double recipe of Flavor-It Sauce. You may store it in a jar in the refrigerator, or in a plastic container in the freezer.

> One tablespoon of Flavor-It Sauce contains 1.4 mgs. of sodium and 15 calories.
> One-half cup of Flavor-It Sauce contains 11 mgs. of sodium.

FLAVOR-IT MINESTRONE SOUP
(8 servings)

1	cup dry kidney beans (uncooked)	1	cup cabbage (shredded)
2	quarts water	1	zucchini (sliced)
1	Tbs. vegetable oil	½	cup green beans
1	medium onion (chopped)	1	cup macaroni (uncooked)
1	stalk celery (chopped)	1	Tbs. parsley flakes
1	can tomato paste (6 oz.)	1	tsp. paprika
¼	cup Flavor-It Sauce (recipe on page 75)	4	whole cloves
		1	tsp. pepper
		½	tsp. marjoram
		½	tsp. oregano

Cover kidney beans with water and soak overnight. Next day: Place beans and water in large pot. Simmer, covered, for 1 hour. While beans are cooking, brown onion and celery in oil in small pan; add tomato paste and Flavor-It Sauce. Cook 5 minutes. Add tomato mixture and all remaining ingredients into pot containing cooked beans and stock. Cook, uncovered, for another ½ hour, until vegetables and macaroni are tender.

This minestrone soup may be frozen.

One serving of Flavor-It minestrone soup contains 24 mgs. of sodium.
148 calories per serving.

COMPARE AND BEWARE:
One serving of canned minestrone soup contains 995 mgs. of sodium.

FLAVOR-IT SWISS STEAK
(4 servings)

- 1 pound flank, round, or chuck steak
- 1 Tbs. vegetable oil
- 4 Tbs. Flavor-It Sauce (recipe on page 75)
- 1/4 cup wine vinegar
- 1/4 cup water
- 1 large onion (sliced)
- 1 green pepper (sliced)
- 2 cloves garlic (crushed)
- 1 bay leaf (crumbled)

Place oil in pan. Brown meat on both sides. Place meat in casserole and add remaining ingredients. Bake covered in 350-degree oven for 1½ hours, or until tender.

One serving of Flavor-It Swiss Steak contains 59 mgs. of sodium.

226 calories per serving.

COMPARE AND BEWARE:
One complete Swiss Steak frozen dinner (10 oz.) contains 965 mgs. of sodium.

FLAVOR-IT GROUND STEAK BELMONT
(4 servings)

- 1 pound lean ground round
- 1 small onion (grated)
- 1 green pepper (diced)
- 1 clove garlic (crushed)
- 2 tsp. parsley flakes
- ½ tsp. pepper
- ¼ tsp. thyme

Place meat in bowl. Add remaining ingredients and mix well. Shape into 4 patties. Place patties on broiler pan and broil on both sides until done.

To Prepare Sauce Belmont:

- 4 Tbs. Flavor-It Sauce (recipe on page 75)
- 1 Tbs. lemon juice
- 2 Tbs. sherry wine
- 1 tsp. dry mustard
- ½ tsp. pepper

Combine Flavor-It Sauce, lemon juice, and wine in a pan. Add dry mustard and pepper. Simmer over low heat for 5 minutes. Serve sauce over broiled beef patties.

One serving of Flavor-It ground steak Belmont contains 53 mgs. of sodium.

179 calories per serving.

COMPARE AND BEWARE:
One serving of dry hamburger seasoning mix prepared with 1 pound of ground beef contains 506 mgs. of sodium.

FLAVOR-IT BEEF STEW
(4 servings)

- 1 pound lean chuck (cut into cubes)
- 1 Tbs. vegetable oil
- 1 cup celery and leaves (½ in. thick slices)
- 1 cup onions (¼ in. thick slices)
- 2 tsp. dill weed
- ½ tsp. pepper
- ½ cup water
- ½ cup Flavor-It Sauce (recipe on page 75)
- 4 Tbs. sour cream

Place oil in pan. Brown meat in hot oil. Set aside. In casserole: Cover bottom with layer of sliced celery, leaves, and onions. Transfer meat to casserole. Sprinkle dill and pepper over meat. Combine water, Flavor-It Sauce, and sour cream and pour over meat. Cook, covered, in 350-degree oven for 1½ hours or until meat is tender.

One serving of Flavor-It beef stew contains 97 mgs. of sodium.

252 calories per serving.

COMPARE AND BEWARE:
One serving of canned beef stew contains 1,007 mgs. of sodium.

FLAVOR-IT TACO FILLING
(4 servings; fills 8 taco shells)

- 1 pound lean ground round
- ½ cup water
- ½ cup Flavor-It Sauce (recipe on page 75)
- 1 tsp. pepper
- 1 tsp. garlic powder
- 2 tsp. chili powder (without salt)

Brown meat in pan. Stir until crumbly. Drain fat. Add remaining ingredients. Bring to a boil. Reduce heat and simmer uncovered for 15 minutes, stirring occasionally. Heat taco shells before serving with filling.

Spoon 3 tablespoons filling into each shell. Add shredded lettuce, chopped tomato, chopped onion, chopped green pepper, or a combination of these vegetables.

One serving of Flavor-It taco filling contains 49 mgs. of sodium.

176 calories per serving.

COMPARE AND BEWARE:
One serving of packaged taco filling contains 2,230 mgs. of sodium.

FLAVOR-IT SPAGHETTI SAUCE AND MEATBALLS
(6 servings)
MEATBALLS

1	pound ground beef	½	tsp. pepper
1	medium onion (grated)	½	tsp. oregano
1	egg yolk	¼	cup Flavor-It Sauce
1	Tbs. parsley flakes		
1	clove garlic (crushed)	2	Tbs. vegetable oil

Combine meat, onion, egg yolk, and seasonings in a bowl. Add Flavor-It Sauce. Shape into small balls. Heat oil in pan and brown meatballs. When browned, remove from pan. Drain. Add meatballs to Flavor-It spaghetti sauce.

FLAVOR-IT SPAGHETTI SAUCE

1	large onion (chopped)	1¼	cups water
1	clove garlic (crushed)	¼	cup Flavor-It Sauce
2	Tbs. vegetable oil	2	bay leaves
1	can tomato paste (6 oz.)	½	tsp. basil
		1	Tbs. oregano
		¼	tsp. pepper

Brown onions and garlic in oil. Add remaining ingredients. Cook, covered, over low heat for 20 minutes. Add browned meatballs and simmer for another 15 minutes. Pour over spaghetti, cooked without salt.

One serving of Flavor-It spaghetti and meatballs contains 68 mgs. of sodium. 361 calories.

COMPARE AND BEWARE:
One serving of canned spaghetti and meatballs contains 1,220 mgs. of sodium.

FLAVOR-IT SPANISH RICE
(6 servings)

- ¾ cup long grain rice (uncooked)
- 2½ cups water
- 2 Tbs. vegetable oil
- 1 small onion (chopped)
- 1 green pepper (chopped)
- 1 stalk celery (chopped)
- ½ cup fresh mushrooms (chopped)
- 4 Tbs. Flavor-It Sauce (recipe on page 75)
- ½ tsp. pepper
- ½ tsp. tarragon

Place rice and water in saucepan. In another pan, heat oil and lightly brown onion, green pepper, celery, and mushrooms. When golden brown, add vegetables to rice and water. Add Flavor-It Sauce, pepper and tarragon. Cook covered for 25 minutes. Do not remove cover or stir.

One serving of Flavor-It Spanish rice contains 17 mgs. of sodium.

152 calories per serving.

COMPARE AND BEWARE:
One serving of Spanish rice prepared with dry packaged mix contains 650 mgs. of sodium.

FLAVOR-IT BAKED BEANS
(4 servings)

- 1 cup dry navy beans
- 3 cups water
- 1 can tomato paste (6 oz.)
- 1 can water (tomato paste can)
- 2 Tbs. Flavor-It Sauce (recipe on page 75)
- 4 Tbs. dark molasses
- 1 Tbs. white vinegar
- 1/4 tsp. dry mustard
- 1/4 tsp. cayenne pepper
- 1/4 tsp. garlic powder

Cover beans with 3 cups water and soak overnight. Next day, add enough additional water to cover beans. Place beans and water in pan. Cover pan and bring liquid to a boil; reduce heat and simmer for 45 minutes or until beans are tender. Place beans in heavy casserole. Add remaining ingredients; cover casserole and bake in 300-degree oven for 1½ hours, until beans are tender and flavorful.

Optional: For extra flavor, add leftover cooked lean meat (beef, lamb, pork) to casserole before baking beans.

> One serving of Flavor-It baked beans contains 36 mgs. of sodium.
> 211 calories per serving.

> COMPARE AND BEWARE:
> One serving of canned baked beans contains 862 mgs. of sodium.

The sodium content and calories do not include any added meat.

FLAVOR-IT RUMP ROAST
(4 servings)

- 1½ pounds rump roast (beef)
- 3 Tbs. flour
- ½ tsp. pepper
- 2 Tbs. vegetable oil
- 2 medium onions (sliced)
- 2 cloves garlic (crushed)
- 2 bay leaves
- 1 tsp. parsley flakes
- ¼ tsp. thyme
- 3 Tbs. Flavor-It Sauce (recipe on page 75)
- 1 can of beer

Sprinkle flour and pepper over meat. Heat oil in pan and brown meat on both sides. Remove meat to roaster. To drippings in pan, add onions and garlic. Lightly brown and pour over meat. Add remaining ingredients. Cook, covered, in 350-degree oven for 1 hour; baste with gravy and continue cooking for another hour, or until meat is tender.

One serving of Flavor-It Rump Roast contains 76 mgs. of sodium.

345 calories per 4 oz. cooked serving.

FLAVOR-IT HERBED MEAT LOAF
(4 servings)

1	pound lean ground round beef	½	tsp. parsley flakes
1	medium onion (grated)	¼	tsp. basil
1	medium potato (raw, grated)	½	tsp. pepper
		¼	cup red wine
		2	Tbs. Flavor-It Sauce (recipe page 75)

Place meat in bowl. Add remaining ingredients and mix well. Shape into a loaf and place on baking pan. Cover pan with aluminum foil and bake in a 350-degree oven for 1 hour.

> One serving contains 48 mgs. of sodium.
> 194 calories per serving.

FLAVOR-IT PAPRIKA PORK CHOPS
(4 servings)

4	loin pork chops (fat trimmed)	1	onion (thin sliced)
1	Tbs. vegetable oil	2	cloves garlic (crushed)
3	Tbs. Flavor-It Sauce (recipe on page 75)	1	tsp. pepper
½	cup water	1	Tbs. paprika

Place oil in pan. Brown chops on both sides. Combine all remaining ingredients and pour over chops. Cover pan and cook over medium heat for 45 minutes or until chops are done.

> One serving contains 34 mgs. of sodium.
> 176 calories per 4 oz. serving.

FLAVOR-IT LEG OF LAMB
(6 servings)

- 2–3 pound leg of lamb (with bone)
- ½ tsp. garlic powder
- 1 tsp. pepper
- ½ tsp. ginger
- ½ tsp. dry mustard
- ½ tsp. chili powder (without salt)
- 1 Tbs. caraway seeds (optional)
- 2 Tbs. lemon juice
- 4 Tbs. Flavor-It Sauce (recipe on page 75)
- ½ cup sherry wine

Combine all herbs and spices. Rub over meat. Place meat in roasting pan and pour over lemon juice. Roast uncovered in 500-degree oven for 20 minutes. Then lower oven temperature to 325 degrees; add Flavor-It Sauce and sherry wine. Cover roasting pan and continue roasting for another 1½ hours or until meat is tender.

One serving of Flavor-It leg-of-lamb contains 82 mgs. of sodium.

255 calories per 4 oz. serving.

FLAVOR-IT CHICKEN MEXICAN
(4 servings)

HOW TO COOK CHICKEN BREASTS

- 2 pounds whole chicken breasts
- 3 cups water
- 2 stalks celery
- 1 carrot, sliced
- 1 whole clove
- 1 onion, sliced
- 3 peppercorns

Place chicken breasts in pot with water and remaining ingredients. Simmer, uncovered, until chicken is tender, about 20–30 minutes. Cool chicken, and dice.

- 2 cups cooked chicken (diced)
- 2 Tbs. vegetable oil
- 1 large onion (diced)
- 1 green pepper (diced)
- ½ pound fresh mushrooms (sliced)
- 1 can tomato paste (6 oz.)
- 2 cups water
- 3 Tbs. Flavor-It Sauce (recipe on page 75)
- 1 tsp. chili powder (*without salt*)
- ½ tsp. pepper

Heat oil in pan and lightly brown onion, green pepper, and mushrooms. Then add remaining ingredients. Cook, covered, over low heat for 30 minutes, stirring occasionally. Just before serving, add chicken and heat thoroughly. Serve over rice, cooked without added salt.

One serving of Flavor-It chicken Mexican contains 113 mgs. of sodium.

341 calories per serving.

FLAVOR-IT FRESH FISH BROIL
(4 servings)

- 4 fish fillets (4 oz. each)
- 1½ tsp. margarine
- ½ tsp. pepper
- ½ tsp. basil
- 1 Tbs. vegetable oil
- 1 small onion (diced)
- ½ cup green pepper (diced)
- ½ cup fresh mushrooms (sliced)
- 4 Tbs. Flavor-It Sauce (recipe on page 75)

Lightly grease broiler pan with margarine. Season fish with pepper and basil. Broil fish until it flakes easily with a fork. Serve with this special sauce.

To prepare sauce:
Place oil in pan. Lightly brown onion, green pepper, and mushrooms. Add Flavor-It Sauce and cook 1 minute more.

Spoon 2 tablespoons of sauce over each broiled fish fillet.

One serving of Flavor-It Fish Broil contains 95 mgs. of sodium.

156 calories per serving.

PART V

A COLOR-CODED GUIDE TO DINING OUT—THE LOW-SODIUM WAY

IF YOUR DOCTOR RECOMMENDS A SODIUM-RESTRICTED DIET, USE THIS GUIDE TO CONSULT WITH YOUR DOCTOR OR DIETITIAN BEFORE DINING OUT.

Working men and women usually eat lunch at a restaurant every day, and many families eat out once a week. Anyone who is trying to "kick the salt habit" needs to know what foods to select from a restaurant menu.

This section gives you an easy COLOR-CODED GUIDE to choosing low-sodium foods when dining out. The foods listed in GREEN are LOWER in sodium content; the foods listed in RED are higher in sodium content.

Read the COLOR-CODED sections for breakfast, lunch, and dinner on the following four pages. Note the special page featuring COLOR-CODED choices at the restaurant salad bar.

This COLOR-CODED GUIDE TO DINING OUT includes the latest authoritative data on the specialties of the leading fast-food restaurants. This information on sodium content (in milligrams) and calories will help you make choices when eating out.

Chinese restaurants prepare most foods with monosodium glutamate, and serve soy sauce at every table.

> *Monosodium glutamate* (referred to as MSG) contains *approximately 500 milligrams of sodium* in one teaspoon.
> *Soy sauce* contains *440 milligrams of sodium* in one teaspoon.

At your request many Chinese restaurants will prepare foods to order *without* monosodium glutamate.

AIRLINE TRAVEL THE LOW-SODIUM WAY

Most airlines have low-sodium meals available for passengers upon request. *Be sure to order* your special meal when you make your ticket reservation. Some airlines require 24-hours advance notice. *AVOID eating the peanuts, bread sticks, cheese spreads, and other snacks served with cocktails and soft drinks during your flight.*

A COLOR-CODED GUIDE TO DINING OUT—
THE LOW-SODIUM WAY
BREAKFAST

Any fruit or fruit juice

Ready-to-eat cereals:
  shredded wheat,
  puffed rice,
  puffed wheat,

Boiled or poached eggs (request that no salt be added in cooking.)

Fried eggs (prepared in sweet butter or vegetable oil)

Breakfast steak

French toast with maple syrup

Toast

Sweet butter, jelly, marmalade, honey

Coffee, tea, milk, cream, half-and-half

Nondairy powdered coffee whitener

Tomato juice (canned)

All other ready-to-eat cereals

Hot cereals (salt is added to cooking water.)

Scrambled eggs, omelet (may be preseasoned)

Fried eggs, scrambled eggs, and omelets are usually prepared in salted margarine or salted butter.

Bacon, Canadian bacon, sausages

Pancakes and waffles

English muffin, doughnuts, muffins

Salted butter, salted margarine

Buttermilk

Do not add salt at the table. One teaspoon of salt contains 2,132 mgs. of sodium.

LUNCH

<table>
<tr><td>

Fruit soups

Sandwiches:
Hamburger made-to-order (request no salt.)
Roast beef (request an inner cut.)
Fresh chicken, sliced
Fresh turkey, sliced
Fresh fish (Ask your waitress if fish is fresh.)
Hard boiled egg, sliced

</td><td>

All other soups

Sandwiches:
Hamburger pre-seasoned with salt
Cheeseburger
Roast beef (end cut)
Chicken salad
Turkey "roll"
Fish sandwiches, (from frozen fish)
Smoked salmon
Canned fish: crab, salmon, sardines, tuna
Egg salad
Processed meats: corned beef, tongue, pastrami, bacon, ham, frankfurters

Sandwich Extras:
Potato chips, coleslaw, potato salad, sauerkraut; pickles, relish, olives, ketchup, chili sauce, tartar sauce, mustard, steak sauce

Cheese Dishes: quiche, soufflé, pizza, Welsh rarebit

</td></tr>
</table>

Salads: See page 96 for salad bar selections
Bread, rolls (plain)   Hamburger buns, frankfurter buns, Kaiser rolls, bread sticks, muffins

A COLOR-CODED GUIDE TO DINING OUT— THE LOW-SODIUM WAY
DINNER
Appetizers

Fresh or canned fruit Oysters Fruit juice	Soups, chopped liver, herring, smoked salmon Tomato juice

Main Course

Lamb chops and steaks made-to-order (request no salt.) Hamburger made-to-order (request no salt.) Roast meats: beef, lamb, pork, veal (request inner cuts.) Veal made-to-order with wine, lemon juice, herbs (request no salt.) Poultry, broiled or roasted (remove skin before eating —skin has been seasoned.) *Fresh fish* only (ask your waitress if fish is fresh; request broiled or baked fish.)	Steaks "tenderized" with meat tenderizer containing sodium Hamburger pre-seasoned with salt Roasts (end cuts) Meats with sauces and gravies Chili, beef stew, pot pies, tacos, pizza Barbecued beef and pork Spareribs Veal Parmesan Veal with sauces (with added salt) Barbecued chicken Fried chicken Poultry in gravy or sauces Frozen fish Fish fried in batter or bread crumbs

For sodium content of lobster, scallops, and shrimp, *see* page 35 of Sodium/Calorie Counter in the Color Coded Shopping Guide.

VEGETABLES

Sweet potatoes Baked potatoes French fried potatoes (ask your waitress if salt has been added.) Fresh or frozen vegetables (request no salt.) Rolls and bread (plain), unsalted melba toast	Creamed potatoes, scalloped potatoes, hash brown potatoes Fresh or frozen vegetables with salt Canned vegetables Bread sticks, crackers, muffins, sweet rolls

Desserts

Fresh or canned fruit Stewed dried fruits Ice cream, sherbet Chocolate sundaes, marshmallow sundaes Angel food cake	Cakes, pies, cookies, puddings, danish pastry Cheese and crackers

Beverages

Coffee, tea, soft drinks, beer, wine, alcoholic beverages	

Do not add salt at the table.
One teaspoon of salt contains 2,132 mgs. of sodium.

SELECT-A-SALAD
AT THE SALAD BAR

MEATS, POULTRY, FISH

Fresh chicken strips Fresh roast beef strips Fresh turkey strips (not from turkey roll)	Bacon, crumbled Bologna, corned beef, ham, pastrami All canned fish; anchovies, crab, sardines, shrimp, tuna

EGGS, CHEESE

Hard boiled eggs	Creamed cottage cheese Cheese strips: American, cheddar, Swiss Grated Parmesan Blue, feta, Roquefort

FRUITS AND VEGETABLES

All fresh fruits All fresh vegetables	All canned vegetables: Artichoke hearts, bean sprouts, beets, corn, garbanzo beans (chick peas), green beans, kidney beans, sauerkraut

SALAD DRESSINGS

Lemon juice Vinegar (white, red, cider Vegetable oils Pepper	All prepared salad dressings Salt

FAST-FOOD RESTAURANTS

Responding to consumer requests for nutrition information, the following restaurant chains have completed nutrient analyses and made them available as a public service. Data from other fast-food chains were not completed at the time of publication and cannot be included.

The sodium content and calories are given in servings. The serving size (weight) is given in grams (g.). Sodium content is in milligrams (mgs.).

McDONALD'S*

ITEM	SERVING WEIGHT (g.)	CALORIES	SODIUM CONTENT (mgs.)
Hamburger	99.3	260	530
Cheeseburger	114.2	300	752
Quarter-Pounder	163.8	420	710
Quarter-Pounder with Cheese	193.4	520	1210
Big Mac	186.7	540	960
Filet-O-Fish	131.3	400	710
French Fries	69.3	210	115
Hashbrown Potatoes	58.1	130	350
Chocolate Shake	288.9	360	320

*Reproduced with permission of McDonald's Corporation. Copyright ©1977, 1978.

FAST-FOOD RESTAURANTS

The sodium content and calories are given in servings. The serving size (weight) is given in grams (g.). Sodium content is in milligrams (mgs.).

McDONALD'S (continued)

ITEM	SERVING WEIGHT (g.)	CALORIES	SODIUM CONTENT (mgs.)
Vanilla Shake	288.7	320	230
Strawberry Shake	292.6	340	265
Apple Pie	91.4	300	415
Cherry Pie	92.4	300	450
McDonald-Land Cookies	63.4	290	330
Hot Fudge Sundae	151.2	290	185
Caramel Sundae	144.6	280	200
Strawberry Sundae	144.2	230	85
Pineapple Sundae	144.1	230	85
Egg McMuffin	132.4	350	915
Hot Cakes with Butter/Syrup	205.9	470	1070
Scrambled Eggs	77.3	160	205
Pork Sausage	48.1	180	465
English Muffin (Buttered)	61.9	190	445

The sodium content and calories are given in servings. The serving size (weight) is given in grams (g.). Sodium content is in milligrams (mgs.).

DAIRY QUEEN*

ITEM	SERVING WEIGHT (g.)	CALORIES	SODIUM CONTENT (mgs.)
Big Brazier Deluxe	213	470	920
Big Brazier Regular	184	457	910
Big Brazier with Cheese	213	553	1435
Brazier with Cheese	121	318	865
Chili Dog	128	330	939
Brazier Dog	99	273	868
Brazier Regular	106	260	576
Super Brazier	298	783	1619
Super Brazier Dog	182	518	1552
Super Brazier Dog with Cheese	203	593	1986
Super Brazier Chili Dog	210	555	1640

*1978 data

FAST-FOOD RESTAURANTS

The sodium content and calories are given in servings. The serving size (weight) is given in grams (g.). Sodium content is in milligrams (mgs.).

PIZZA HUT*

THIN'N CRISPY PIZZA (2 slices from 13" pie)

	SERVING	CALORIES	SODIUM (mgs.)
Standard Cheese	one	340	1000
SuperStyle Cheese	one	410	2000
Standard Pepperoni	one	370	1000
SuperStyle Pepperoni	one	430	2000
Standard Pork with Mushrooms	one	380	2000
SuperStyle Pork with Mushrooms	one	450	2000
Supreme	one	400	2000
Super Supreme	one	510	2000

*1979 data

The sodium content and calories are given in servings. The serving size (weight) is given in grams (g.). Sodium content is in milligrams (mgs.).

WENDY'S*

ITEM	SERVING WEIGHT (g.)	CALORIES	SODIUM CONTENT (mgs.)
Hamburger (single)	200	472	774
Hamburger (double)	285	669	980
Hamburger (triple)	360	853	1217
Single Cheese	240	577	1085
Double Cheese	325	797	1414
Triple Cheese	400	1036	1848
Chili	250	229	1065
French Fries	120	327	112
Frosty	250	391	247

*1979 data

FAST-FOOD RESTAURANTS

The sodium content and calories are given in servings. The serving size (weight) is given in ounces (oz.). Sodium content is in milligrams (mgs.).

ARBY'S*

ITEM	SERVING WEIGHT	CALORIES	SODIUM CONTENT (mgs.)
Sandwiches			
Roast Beef	5	350	880
Beef & Cheese	6	450	1220
Super Roast Beef	9.75	620	1420
Swiss King	9.25	660	1585
Ham 'N Cheese	5.50	380	1350
Turkey	6	410	1060
Turkey Deluxe	8.51	510	1220
Club	9	560	1610

KENTUCKY FRIED CHICKEN**

3-Piece Dinner:
Chicken (3 pieces), Mashed Potatoes and Gravy, Cole Slaw, and Roll.

Original Recipe	15.0 oz.	830	2285
Extra Crispy	15.4 oz.	950	1915

*1979 data   **1976 data

BURGER KING*

ITEM	SERVING	CALORIES	SODIUM CONTENT (mgs.)
**Hamburger	one	290	525
**Cheeseburger	one	350	730
**Double Cheeseburger	one	530	990
**Whopper Jr.	one	370	560
**Whopper Jr. with Cheese	one	420	785
**Whopper	one	630	990
**Whopper with Cheese	one	740	1435
**Double Beef Whopper	one	850	1080
**Double Beef Whopper with Cheese	one	950	1535
**French Fries	one	210	230
**Onion Rings	one	270	450
Apple Pie	one	240	335
Chocolate Shake	one	340	280
Vanilla Shake	one	340	320

*1979 data
**To reduce sodium contents, sandwiches may be ordered without pickles; french fries and onion rings without added salt.

PART VI
DRUGSTORE SODIUM-SHOPPING GUIDE

> CAUTION: If you are taking *any* medication prescribed by your physician for any illness—particularly high blood pressure or coronary heart disease—you should *ALWAYS* consult your physician before taking any over-the-counter nonprescription drug.

You may automatically pop a tablet into your mouth for relief of upset stomach, heartburn, or indigestion. If you need a laxative or cough medicine, you go to the drugstore and make your own selection of a popular over-the-counter remedy. You probably don't think of checking with your doctor, even though you may be on a sodium-restricted diet.

However, if you are trying to reduce your sodium intake, you should be aware that *many of these products contain sodium*—large amounts in some cases. Some manufacturers even print warnings on their labels that say "Do not use this product if you are on a sodium-restricted diet."

Other products are relatively low in sodium content. What is important to remember is that even though the sodium content of one tablet or teaspoon is low, you must multiply each dosage by the number of times you take it each day. That total amount must be figured in your total sodium intake per day.

Also remember that many products are taken over long periods of time, and thus have a longterm effect on the total amount of sodium you are consuming.

The charts on the following two pages will make you aware of the sodium contents of products that relieve upset stomach and indigestion. The third chart includes laxatives and cough syrups.

DRUGSTORE SODIUM

Read across these pages to find the sodium

PRODUCT	SODIUM CONTENT OF 1 TABLET OR 1 TEASPOON

ASPIRIN—An aspirin tablet containing aspirin alone (*without any added ingredients*) usually does not contain sodium.

ANTACIDS:

ALKA-SELTZER EFFERVESCENT ANTACID	276 mgs. per tablet (dissolved in water)
ALKA-SELTZER EFFERVESCENT PAIN RELIEVER AND ANTACID	521 mgs. per tablet (dissolved in water)
BISODOL	.036 mgs. per tablet
BRIOSCHI	710 mgs. per capful (dissolved in water)
BROMO-SELTZER	758 mgs. per capful (dissolved in water)
CHOOZ	3.15 mgs. per gum tablet
DI-GEL	10.6 mgs. per tablet

**Sodium is listed in milligrams.

SHOPPING GUIDE
content of the following products:

MANUFACTURERS' RECOMMENDED DOSAGE*	SODIUM CONTENT** OF RECOMMENDED DOSAGE
1–2 tablets	1 tablet—276 mgs. 2 tablets—552 mgs.
2 tablets	2 tablets—1042 mgs.
2–4 tablets	2 tablets—.072 4 tablets—.144
1–2 capfuls	1 capful—710 mgs. 2 capfuls—1420 mgs.
1–2 capfuls	1 capful—758 mgs. 2 capfuls—1516 mgs.
1–2 tablets	1 tablet—3.15 mgs. 2 tablets—6.30 mgs.
2 tablets	2 tablets—21.2 mgs.

*Manufacturers' recommended dosage taken from product label.

DRUGSTORE SODIUM

Read across these pages to find the sodium

PRODUCT	SODIUM CONTENT OF 1 TABLET OR 1 TEASPOON
GELUSIL	9 mgs. per tablet 8 mgs. per teaspoon
GELUSIL M	10 mgs. per tablet 9 mgs. per teaspoon
MAALOX LIQUID (reg.)	2.5 mgs. per teaspoon
MAALOX No. 1 TABLET	.84 mgs. per tablet
MAALOX No. 2 TABLET	1.95 mgs. per tablet
MYLANTA	.79 mgs. per tablet 11.7 mgs. per teaspoon
MYLANTA-II	1.5 mgs. per tablet 4–10 mgs. per teaspoon
RIOPAN	.7 mgs. per tablet
ROLAIDS	53 mgs. per tablet
TUMS	2.7 mgs. per tablet

SHOPPING GUIDE

content of the following products:

MANUFACTURERS' RECOMMENDED DOSAGE	SODIUM CONTENT OF RECOMMENDED DOSAGE
2 tablets	2 tablets—18 mgs.
2 teaspoons	2 teaspoons—16 mgs.
2 tablets	2 tablets—20 mgs.
2 teaspoons	2 teaspoons—18 mgs.
2–4 teaspoons	2 teaspoons—5.0 mgs. 4 teaspoons—10 mgs.
2–4 tablets	2 tablets—1.68 mgs. 4 tablets—3.36 mgs.
1–2 tablets	1 tablet—1.95 mgs. 2 tablets—3.90 mgs.
1–2 tablets	1 tablet—.79 mgs. 2 tablets—1.58 mgs.
1–2 teaspoons	1 teaspoon—11.7 mgs. 2 teaspoons—23.4 mgs.
1–2 tablets	1 tablet—1.5 mgs. 2 tablets—3.0 mgs.
1–2 teaspoons	1 teaspoon—4–10 mgs. 2 teaspoons—8–20 mgs.
1–2 tablets	1 tablet—.7 mgs.
1–2 tablets	1 tablet—53 mgs. 2 tablets—106 mgs.
1–2 tablets	1 tablet—2.7 mgs. 2 tablets—5.4 mgs.

DRUGSTORE SODIUM

Read across these pages to find the sodium

PRODUCT	SODIUM CONTENT OF 1 TABLET OR 1 TEASPOON
LAXATIVES:	
COLACE (100 mg)	5.2 mgs. per capsule
PERI-COLACE	5.2 mgs. per capsule
DIALOSE/ DIALOSE PLUS*	sodium free
DORBANTYL	2.6 mgs. per capsule
DUAL FORMULA FEEN-A-MINT	5.2 mgs. per chewable tablet
METAMUCIL	negligible sodium in 1 teaspoon
METAMUCIL INSTANT MIX	**250 mgs. per packet (dissolved in water)**
SENOKOT S	2.6 mgs. per tablet
COUGH MEDICATIONS:	
CHLOR-TRIMETON EXPECTORANT	13.4 mgs. per teaspoon
TUSSAR-2	34.7 mgs. per teaspoon
VICKS COUGH SYRUP	53.5 mgs. per teaspoon
VICKS FORMULA 44	66.8 mgs. per teaspoon

Data on drugstore products were obtained from: *Handbook of Nonprescription Drugs* (Fifth Edition), American Pharmaceutical Association, Washington, D.C., December 1977.

---

*Data from July 1, 1979 Bulletin from Stuart Pharmaceuticals.

SHOPPING GUIDE

content of the following products

MANUFACTURERS' RECOMMENDED DOSAGE*	SODIUM CONTENT OF RECOMMENDED DOSAGE
2 capsules	2 capsules—10.4 mgs.
1–2 capsules	1 capsule—5.2 mgs. 2 capsules—10.4 mgs.
1 capsule	1 capsule—sodium free
2 capsules	2 capsules—5.2 mgs.
1–2 tablets	1 tablet—5.2 mgs. 2 tablets—10.4 mgs.
1 teaspoon	1 teaspoon—negligible sodium
1 packet	1 packet—250 mgs.
1–2 tablets	1 tablet—2.6 mgs. 2 tablets—5.2 mgs.
1 teaspoon	1 teaspoon—13.4 mgs.
1 teaspoon	1 teaspoon—34.7 mgs.
1 teaspoon	1 teaspoon—53.5 mgs.
1–2 teaspoons	1 teaspoon—66.8 mgs. 2 teaspoons—133.6 mgs.

Consultant: Dr. Allan S. Hoffman, Assistant Director, Center for Bio-Engineering, University of Washington, Seattle, Washington.

PART VII

THE DOCTOR ANSWERS QUESTIONS ON SALT, BLOOD PRESSURE, AND YOUR HEALTH

By Abby G. Abelson, M.D.

Americans are becoming increasingly aware of the possible effects of sodium on their health, and are seeking information from their doctors concerning their diet and their health. Some of the most frequently asked questions are answered on the following pages by Abby G. Abelson, M.D.

CONSULT YOUR OWN PHYSICIAN FOR DIET RECOMMENDATIONS FOR YOUR INDIVIDUAL HEALTH NEEDS.

Q. HOW DOES SALT AFFECT MY BODY?
A. Table salt is a combination of two elements: sodium and chloride. Sodium is the most important element in the control of water balance in the body. It is important that proper water balance be maintained to help assure that all cells of the body function normally. The body controls water balance by keeping the sodium in the blood at a constant level. The amount of sodium in the blood regulates the amount of fluid in the blood vessels and body tissues.

Q. HOW IS THE SODIUM LEVEL REGULATED IN THE BODY?
A. The sodium balance is regulated by the kidneys. The kidneys have several mechanisms to maintain this sodium balance. In a healthy body, the kidneys balance the intake of sodium from the foods we eat by excreting an equal amount into the urine. (A small amount of sodium is also lost in sweat and in the stool.)

Q. WHAT IF THE BODY DOES NOT MAINTAIN A PROPER BALANCE OF SODIUM?
A. It can result in many health problems, including high blood pressure.

Q. HOW DOES SODIUM INFLUENCE BLOOD PRESSURE?
A. The amount of sodium retained by the kidneys determines how much water remains in the body. Much of this fluid that is not excreted circulates inside the blood vessels. If the kidneys retain too much sodium, excess fluid accumulates. This excess fluid in the vessels exerts a greater push against the vessel walls, creating a higher pressure.

Q. WHAT IS BLOOD PRESSURE?
A. Blood pressure is the force needed to push blood through your blood vessels.

Q. WHAT IS HIGH BLOOD PRESSURE?
A. High blood pressure is a sustained increase in pressure in the arteries, the tubes that carry blood from the heart to the various parts of the body. Elevated pressure in these vessels means that the blood flow pushes with greater force against the walls of the vessels as your heart pumps blood through them.

Q. WHAT IS HYPERTENSION?
A. Hypertension is the medical term for high blood pressure.

Q. IS HYPERTENSION A MAJOR HEALTH PROBLEM?
A. Definitely yes! Here are the latest figures from the National Heart, Lung, and Blood Institute:

1. "Almost 35 million persons in the United States are estimated to have definite high blood pressure and face significant risks of heart attack, stroke, and kidney failure." 2. "In addition, approximately 25 *million persons* in the United States are estimated to have borderline high blood pressure and likely require regular surveillance." 3. Therefore, "Nearly 60 million American adults are determined to be at risk of developing blood vessel disease with subsequent heart attack, stroke, or kidney failure due to elevated blood pressure." One out of every four Americans faces these serious health risks. That certainly makes it a major health problem!

Q. HOW DO I KNOW IF I HAVE HIGH BLOOD PRESSURE?
A. You can't feel high blood pressure. While most other diseases have symptoms such as a cough or a pain, high blood pressure has no symptoms until it becomes quite serious. The only way you can know if you have high blood pressure is to get your blood pressure measured.

Q. WHERE CAN I GET MY BLOOD PRESSURE TAKEN?
A. You can get your blood pressure measured by your doctor, at your local health clinic, or by special machines available in some shopping areas and airports. You can even buy instruments to take your blood pressure in your own home.

Q. DOES MY BLOOD PRESSURE ALWAYS STAY THE SAME?
A. No. Your blood pressure tends to vary. One blood-pressure check is not enough. You should get a series of readings to establish whether or not you have chronic high blood pressure.

Q. WHAT DO THE NUMBERS MEAN IN THE BLOOD-PRESSURE READING?
A. The blood-pressure reading has two parts, a high number and a low number. The higher number is the *systolic pressure* and the lower number is the *diastolic pressure*.

Q. WHAT DOES "SYSTOLIC" AND "DIASTOLIC" PRESSURE MEAN?
A. Because the walls of the arterial vessels are muscular and elastic, they can stretch to accommodate the highs and lows of blood pressure. With each heartbeat the pressure in the arteries goes up, and in between heartbeats, the pressure goes down. The higher pressure, during the heartbeat, is the *systolic* pressure and the lower pressure, in between heartbeats, is the *diastolic* pressure. If your doctor tells you that your blood pressure is 150 over 93, the systolic is 150 and the diastolic is 93.

Q. WHAT IS A NORMAL BLOOD PRESSURE?
A. There is a wide range of normal blood pressures. An average blood pressure reading, for example, is 120 over 80 (120/80), but any blood pressure up to 140 over 90 (140/90) would be considered normal for the adult population.

Q. WHAT IS CONSIDERED A HIGH BLOOD PRESSURE?
A. Blood pressures over 160 over 95 (160/95) are considered definitely high. Blood pressure readings between 140 over 90 (140/90) and 160 over 95 (160/95) are considered "borderline hypertensive."

Q. WHAT CAN HIGH BLOOD PRESSURE DO TO MY BODY?
A. It can affect all of your vital organs—your heart, your brain, and your kidneys.

Q. WHAT HAPPENS IF HYPERTENSION ISN'T TREATED?
A. If left untreated, hypertension can go on for fifteen or twenty years before damage to vital organs becomes apparent. Although hypertension may not cause symptoms during these years, your body organs are being affected. Often the first symptom people feel is the result of involvement of one of these organs.

Q. CAN HIGH BLOOD PRESSURE SHORTEN MY LIFE?
A. Yes, even a person with "borderline" high blood pressure, left untreated, runs more than twice the risk of having a heart attack and nearly four times the risk of having a stroke than a person with normal blood pressure.

Q. WILL TREATMENT HELP?
A. Treatment of high blood pressure reduces the risk of coronary heart disease, congestive heart failure, heart attacks, kidney failure, stroke, and eye changes.

Q. HOW DOES HIGH BLOOD PRESSURE AFFECT THE HEART?
A. Hypertension affects the heart in a number of ways. Because the heart has to pump against a high pressure in the arteries, it has to work extra hard. At first the heart muscle becomes thicker, just as the muscle of your arm gets bigger if you lift weights. After several years, however, your heart muscle cannot get any thicker, and it starts to get big and weak and floppy. That is when congestive heart failure may set in.

Q. WHAT IS CONGESTIVE HEART FAILURE?
A. Congestive failure occurs when the heart cannot pump out all the fluid, which tends to back up and accumulate in the lungs and in the legs. People with congestive heart failure may have shortness of breath and swelling in their legs as symptoms.

Q. WHAT CAUSES CONGESTIVE HEART FAILURE?
A. While many diseases can cause congestive heart failure, seventy-five percent of the cases are caused by hypertension. There is six times more congestive failure in hypertensive patients than in those with normal pressures.

A study of over five thousand hypertensive patients by the Heart Disease Epidemiology Study in Framingham, Massachusetts, concluded that

> early vigorous and sustained control of elevated blood pressure...appears the chief means for preventing congestive heart failure in the general population.

Q. WHAT IS TREATMENT FOR CONGESTIVE HEART FAILURE?
A. A low-sodium diet is often prescribed, along with medications.

Q. HOW ELSE DOES HYPERTENSION AFFECT THE HEART?
A. In addition to congestive heart failure, hypertension causes coronary heart disease.

Q. WHAT IS CORONARY HEART DISEASE?
A. Coronary heart disease is caused by atherosclerosis of the blood vessels that carry blood to the heart muscle.

Q. WHAT IS ATHEROSCLEROSIS?
A. Atherosclerosis is a process in which fatty materials are deposited on the inside of arteries, making them narrower.

Q. HOW IS ATHEROSCLEROSIS RELATED TO HYPERTENSION?
A. The process of atherosclerosis is speeded up by the presence of hypertension.

Q. WHAT ARE THE EFFECTS OF CORONARY HEART DISEASE?
A. Coronary heart disease causes heart attacks, heart pain (angina pectoris), or sudden death.

Q. I HAVE HIGH BLOOD PRESSURE. IF I LOWER MY BLOOD PRESSURE, CAN I LOWER MY CHANCES OF GETTING HEART DISEASE?
A. Yes. Coronary heart disease is less frequent in a population with normal blood pressures, and is significantly reduced by treatment of hypertension. The sooner high blood pressure is detected and brought under control, the more likely it is that a reduction in coronary heart disease can be achieved.
The Framingham Study concluded:
> Few conditions so easily detected and readily controlled are more potent than hypertension as a menace to health.

Q. CAN HIGH BLOOD PRESSURE CAUSE A STROKE?
A. Hypertension is the key factor in determining the risk of stroke. Strokes happen when the blood vessels in the brain are severely affected by atherosclerosis, so that there is a decrease in blood supply to an area of the brain. This decreased blood supply can result in paralysis, loss of speech, or visual disturbance.

There is strong evidence that the key to prevention of strokes is "early detection and control of hypertension." The American Heart Association states that

> even modest blood pressure elevations—at any age in either sex—may adversely affect stroke risk.

Q. WHAT OTHER PARTS OF THE BODY CAN BE AFFECTED BY HIGH BLOOD PRESSURE?
A. High blood pressure can affect the kidneys by damaging the small blood vessels within them. Complete kidney failure can be caused by hypertension.

Your eyes can also be affected. The small blood vessels in the back of your eye are especially sensitive to the effects of elevated pressure. These will be the earliest blood vessels to be affected, so your doctor will keep a close watch on your eyes in physical examinations.

Q. WHAT CAUSES HIGH BLOOD PRESSURE?
A. In most cases of hypertension the cause is unknown. In fact, over 90% of patients diagnosed with hypertension are labeled by doctors as having "essential" or "primary" hypertension—meaning hypertension of unknown cause.

In only about 10% of the cases is the elevated blood pressure due to another underlying disease.

Q. CAN EATING TOO MUCH SODIUM CAUSE HYPERTENSION?
A. A great deal of research is being done to determine the cause or causes of this disease.

At the present time much evidence seems to point to excessive sodium retention within the body as a common condition in many types of hypertension.

Although it has not been firmly established that there is a causal relationship in humans between sodium intake and hypertension, studies in animals have shown that excessive salt intake in early life, operating together with a hereditary predisposition, may lead to the development of hypertension. In one widely reported study by Dr. Lewis K. Dahl, people more often had hypertension when they reported high salt intake.

The American Heart Association states:
> There is increasing evidence that current levels of sodium intake in the U.S. contribute as one of the multiple factors in the etiology [causes] of hypertension.

The American Heart Association concludes:
> Information available to date from human and experimental studies suggests that it is prudent to AVOID EXCESSIVE SODIUM IN THE DIET.

Q. WHAT OTHER FACTORS PLAY A ROLE IN HIGH BLOOD PRESSURE?
A. Heredity, body weight, life-style, stress, other minerals in the diet, and hormones circulating in the bloodstream are factors which seem to play a causal role in hypertension.

Q. I'M A VERY CALM PERSON. HOW CAN I HAVE HYPERTENSION IF I'M NOT TENSE?
A. Many people confuse nervous tension with hypertension, the medical term for high blood pressure. These terms are completely unrelated. Although blood pressure does tend to rise when you're nervous or excited, in normal people it goes down again after the stress is over. Sustained, or chronic, high blood pressure is abnormal.

You can't judge your blood pressure by how tense or calm you feel. The only way to know if your blood pressure is high is to have it measured.

Q. WHO IS MORE LIKELY TO HAVE HYPERTENSION?
A. People in certain population groups are much more likely to have hypertension, and they should have careful regular blood pressure measurements.

Read the following seven questions and answers for the population groups who are more likely to get high blood pressure.

Q. ARE BLACK AMERICANS MORE LIKELY TO GET HIGH BLOOD PRESSURE?
A. Black Americans are fifty percent more likely to have high blood pressure than whites. It is the largest cause of death among blacks.

Hypertension is one condition that contributes to stroke and heart attack, and blacks have more strokes at an earlier age, and with more severe results.

Q. MY FATHER HAS HIGH BLOOD PRESSURE. AM I MORE LIKELY TO GET IT?
A. Heredity seems to contribute to the likelihood of developing hypertension. If your parents and other relatives have had high blood pressure, the chances increase of your developing it, too.

If you have high blood pressure, your children may develop it. Children, as well as adults, should have regular blood pressure checks.

Q. DOES AGE INCREASE MY CHANCES OF GETTING HIGH BLOOD PRESSURE?

A. Aging contributes to a tendency to develop increased blood pressure. Increased stiffness of the walls of the large arteries—often a natural consequence of aging—tends to raise blood pressure.

Q. IS HIGH BLOOD PRESSURE MORE COMMON IN MEN?
A. In a study of a million Americans from 1973 through 1975, higher blood pressures were found in men when compared with women, in all racial groups, until the age of fifty.

Q. WHAT ABOUT WOMEN AFTER MENOPAUSE?
A. After menopause, a woman's chances of having high blood pressure become greater than a man's. Even women who have had normal blood pressures their entire lives should have their blood pressure checked regularly after menopause because of the greater risk.

Q. DOES TAKING "THE PILL" AFFECT MY CHANCES OF DEVELOPING HIGH BLOOD PRESSURE?
A. Some women who take birth control pills have a higher risk of developing hypertension. Those women on the pill who are also overweight, have been hypertensive during a pregnancy, have a family history of hypertension, or have mild kidney disease, are especially likely to develop an elevated blood pressure. Your blood pressure should be checked before you start taking the pill and then about twice a year while you're taking it.

Q. ARE PREGNANT WOMEN SUSCEPTIBLE TO HIGH BLOOD PRESSURE?
A. Pregnant women may develop high blood pressure, either during pregnancy or after delivery. That is why doctors closely watch a woman's blood pressure during pregnancy.

REMEMBER—the fact that you are not in any of the groups just discussed does not rule out the possibility that you may have high blood pressure. You should still have you blood pressure measured to determine whether or not you are hypertensive.

Q. CAN HIGH BLOOD PRESSURE BE CURED?
A. *High blood pressure cannot be cured.* Until doctors and other researchers can discover a cause for the disease, a cure is impossible. But the important thing is that HIGH BLOOD PRESSURE CAN BE CONTROLLED WITH PROPER TREATMENT.

Several studies have shown that lowering blood pressures of hypertensive patients through careful treatment can decrease their risk of heart failure, kidney failure, stroke, and coronary heart disease.

Q. WHAT IS THE TREATMENT FOR HIGH BLOOD PRESSURE?

A. *Treatment for high blood pressure should be carried out under your doctor's supervision.* A basic treatment for high blood pressure usually includes dietary restriction of sodium. Sodium restriction alone may or may not lower your blood pressure into the normal range, but a restriction to less than two thousand milligrams of sodium daily has been shown to significantly reduce blood pressure in hypertensive patients.

Often, sodium restriction alone is the only therapy required to bring a hypertensive blood pressure into the normal range. Sodium restriction usually requires at least a few weeks of following a low-sodium diet before the blood-pressure-lowering effect can be appreciated.

Q. WILL LOSING WEIGHT HELP LOWER MY BLOOD PRESSURE?

A. Yes, overweight patients who lose at least fifteen pounds often develop a lower blood pressure with the weight loss. In addition, weight reduction lessens the workload of the heart, which is overworked when having to pump against elevated arterial pressure.

Q. WHAT IF MY BLOOD PRESSURE CAN'T BE CONTROLLED WITH DIET ALONE?

A. If your blood pressure does not lower into the normal range with dietary management alone, or if your doctor feels that your blood pressure is too high to respond simply to sodium restriction in your diet, your doctor will put you on medication.

Q. WHAT MEDICATIONS WILL HELP LOWER MY BLOOD PRESSURE?

A. "Water pills," or diuretics, are probably the first type of medication that your doctor will try. Diuretics act to increase your kidneys' excretion of sodium and water, thereby lowering your body's total amount of fluid. This results in less fluid in the blood vessels, thereby reducing the pressure on the vessel walls.

Other medications that may be prescribed influence the narrowing of the vessels.

As with any other medication, the blood-pressure-lowering drugs have different effects on different people. In most cases of essential hypertension, your blood pressure will be lowered, but it may take a period of time before your doctor finds the medicine or combination of medicines that works for you. And remember, *medications for blood pressure work only if taken regularly and according to your doctor's instructions.*

Q. CAN'T I JUST TAKE A PILL FOR MY HIGH BLOOD PRESSURE AND NOT WORRY ABOUT STAYING ON A LOW-SODIUM DIET?

A. No. Take your pills as prescribed, but watch your sodium, too.

You are working against the medication if you add a large salt load to your diet, because diuretics act by eliminating sodium and water through the kidneys. Too often patients are believed to have "resistant hypertension," or hypertension that fails to respond to treatment, when it becomes clear that the patient is eating excessive salt. This high sodium intake could completely nullify the sodium-and-water balance of the diuretics or reverse the antihypertensive effect of other medications.

Q. IS A LOW-SALT DIET PRESCRIBED FOR ANY OTHER MEDICAL CONDITION?

A. Yes. It is often recommended by doctors as a treatment for Méniére's disease. This is a problem within the inner ear, which results in episodes of dizziness, ringing in the ear, and decreased hearing. Although the exact cause of the disease is unknown, the symptoms are thought to result from fluid pressure buildup in the inner ear. Many doctors prescribe a low-salt diet and/or diuretics, as the initial medical treatment for Méniére's disease, hoping to decrease the fluid pressure in the inner ear and reduce the frequency or severity of the "attacks."

Q. CAN I USE "SALT SUBSTITUTES" INSTEAD OF ORDINARY TABLE SALT ON MY LOW-SODIUM DIET?

A. Salt substitutes should only be used with the permission of your doctor, because many salt substitutes contain potassium, an element in delicate balance in your body that may affect a medication your doctor has prescribed. Ask his or her advice about salt substitutes.

Q. HOW CAN I STAY ON A LOW-SODIUM DIET WHEN THE FOODS ARE SO TASTELESS WITHOUT SALT?

A. Since most people are used to eating their foods with too much salt, their taste buds become accustomed to too much salt. However, people who have faithfully followed low-sodium diets for several weeks find that foods which they previously considered to be lightly salted now taste heavily salted. (The taste buds involved with sensing salt adjust to the lower level of sodium in the diet by becoming more sensitive to the taste of salt.) You will, after a time, get used to the lower level of sodium without a loss of food flavor.

Editor's Note: You can learn imaginative ways to prepare tasty family meals without salt, by consulting the FLAVOR-MAGIC CHART on page 68 and using FLAVOR-IT SAUCE in the recipes on pages 75 and 76.

Q. HOW LONG WILL I NEED TREATMENT FOR MY HIGH BLOOD PRESSURE?
A. Many people are under the mistaken impression that once they start treatment and their blood pressure returns to normal levels, they are cured. Because these patients may not have had any symptoms in the first place, they feel fine and may stop taking their medication.

This is a terrible, and potentially fatal, error. If you stop treatment, your blood pressure will most likely go up again! People with high blood pressure should control it every day by following their diet, taking regularly any medication that the doctor prescribes, and doing what the doctor recommends.

Q. CAN I LIVE A NORMAL LIFE WITH HIGH BLOOD PRESSURE?
A. Hypertension is a disease that you may have for the rest of your life, but millions of people are living happy and productive lives by controlling their blood pressure. They are protecting themselves against the complications of hypertension with careful treatment.

Remember, because high blood pressure is a long-standing disease requiring daily treatment, you are the most important "doctor" of your blood pressure.

You can save your own life.

Abby G. Abelson, M.D., in Cleveland, Ohio, is a graduate of Case Western Reserve University School of Medicine.

BIBLIOGRAPHY

COMPOSITION OF FOODS—Dairy and Egg Products: Raw, Processed, Prepared. Agriculture Handbook No. 8-1. United States Department of Agriculture, Washington, D.C., revised November 1976.

COMPOSITION OF FOODS—Raw, Processed, Prepared. Watt, Bernice K., and Annabel L. Merrill, Agriculture Handbook No. 8. United States Department of Agriculture, Washington, D.C., October 1975.

COMPOSITION OF FOODS—Spices and Herbs: Raw, Processed, Prepared. Agriculture Handbook No. 8-2. United States Department of Agriculture, Washington, D.C., revised January 1977.

DIETARY GOALS FOR THE UNITED STATES. Second Edition. Select Committee on Nutrition and Human Needs, United States Senate. U. S. Government Printing Office, Washington, D.C., December 1977.

FOOD VALUES OF PORTIONS COMMONLY USED. Bowes and Church, Twelfth Edition. Revised by Charles F. Church and Helen N. Church, J. B. Lippincott Co., Philadelphia, 1975.

NUTRITIVE VALUE OF AMERICAN FOODS. Adams, Catherine F. In Common Units. Agriculture Handbook No. 456. United States Department of Agriculture, Washington, D. C., issued November 1975.

The sodium content of some foods has been supplied by manufacturers, or taken directly from nutrition information printed on the product label.

MEDICAL BIBLIOGRAPHY

American Heart Association publications:
Coronary Risk Handbook, 1973.

Diet and Coronary Heart Disease, 1978.

Heart Facts, 1979.

High Blood Pressure, and How to Control It. Pamphlet. 1974.

Stroke Risk Handbook, 1974.

Black, Henry R., M.D. "Nonpharmacologic Therapy for Hypertension." *The American Journal of Medicine,* Vol. 66, pp. 837–842, May 1979.

Crane, M. G. et al. "Hypertension, Oral Contraceptive Agents, and Conjugated Estrogens." *Annals of Internal Medicine,* 74, pp. 13–21, 1971.

Dahl, Lewis K. "Salt and Hypertension." *American Journal of Clinical Nutrition,* 25, pp. 231–244, February 1972.

Dustan, Harriet, M. D. *"What Every Woman Should Know About High Blood Pressure."* Reprinted from *Family Health Magazine,* American Heart Association.

Gifford, R. W. "Managing Hypertension." *Postgraduate Medicine,* Vol., 61, No. 3, pp. 153–163, 1977.

Gifford, R. W. and Tarazi, R. G. "Resistant Management: Diagnosis and Management." *Annals of Internal Medicine,* 88, pp. 661–665, 1978.

Harrison's Textbook of Internal Medicine, Wintrobe et al. McGraw–Hill, Inc., 8th Edition, 1977.

Kannel, W. B., Castelli, W. R., McNamara, P. M. et al. "Role of Blood Pressure in the Development of Congestive Heart Failure. The Framingham Study." *New England Journal of Medicine,* Vol. 287, No. 16, pp. 781–787, 1972.

Kannel, W. B., Schwartz, M. J., and McNamara, P. M. "Blood Pressure and Risk of Coronary Heart Disease: The Framingham Study." *Diseases of the Chest,* Vol. 56, No. 43, 1969.

Kannel, W. B., Wolfe, P. A., Verter, J. et. al. "Epidemiologic Assessment of the Role of Blood Pressure in Stroke: The Framingham Study." *Journal of the American Medical Association,* Vol. 202, No. 1028, 1967.

Lieberman, E. "Hypertension in Childhood and Adolescence." *Ciba Clinical Symposia,* Vol. 30, No. 3, 1978.

National Heart, Lung, and Blood Institute, National High Blood Pressure Education Program, National Institutes of Health, U. S. Department of Health, Education and Welfare: *Report of the Joint National Committee on*
  1. *Detection, Evaluation, and Treatment of High Blood Pressure, 1978.*
  2. *High Blood Pressure and You, 1979.*
  3. *New Hypertension Prevalence Data, 1978.*

Page, L. B. and Sidd J. J. "Medical Management of Primary Hypertension." *New England Journal of Medicine,* Vol. 287, Nos. 19, 20, and 21, pp. 960–967, 1018–1023, 1074–1080, 1972.

Stamler, J., Stamler, R., and Riedlinger, W. F. et al. "Hypertension Screening of One Million Americans." Community Health Evaluation Clinic Program 1973–1975. *Journal of the American Medical Association*, Vol. 235, No. 2299, 1976.

Stone, R. J. and De Leo, J. "Psychotherapeutic Control of Hypertension." *New England Journal of Medicine*, Vol. 294, No. 2, pp. 80–84, 1976.

Tarazi, R. C. "The Heart in Hypertension: Its Load and Its Role." *Hospital Practice*, pp. 31–40. December 1975.

Vander, A. J., Sherman, J. H., and Luciano, D. S. *Human Physiology*, pp. 280–282, McGraw–Hill, 1975.

Veterans Administration Cooperative Study Group on Antihypertensive Agents. "Effects of Treatment on Morbidity in Hypertension: I." *Journal of the American Medical Association*, Vol. 202, No. 1028, 1967.

Veterans Administration Cooperative Study Group on Antihypertensive Agents. "Effects of Treatment on Morbidity in Hypertension: II." *Journal of the American Medical Association*, Vol. 213, No. 1143, 1970.

Weiss, N. S. "Relationship of High Blood Pressure to Headache, Epistaxis, and Selected Other Symptoms." *New England Journal of Medicine*, Vol. 287, No. 13, pp. 631–633, 1972.

Wilkins, R. W., Hollander W., and Choranian, A. V. "Evaluation of Hypertensive Patients." *CIBA Clinical Symposia*, Vol. 24, No. 2, 1972.

Wotman, S., Mandel. I. D., Thompson, R. H. et al, "Salivary Electrolytes and Salt Taste Thresholds in Hypertension." *Journal of Chronic Disease*, Vol. 20, Nos. 833–840, 1967.

About the Authors

A graduate of the Department of Nutrition of Case Western Reserve University, Janet James is well known in the northern Ohio area as a popular lecturer and demonstrator on easy-to-prepare gourmet foods.

As former head of the Consumer Services Division of a major supermarket chain, she became aware of the special diet needs of many consumers. She is co-author of *"Better Meals for YOU with Low-Calorie Gourmet Recipes,"* endorsed by the Greater Cleveland Diabetic Association.

Her first book, *Quick Cuisine*, was the result of her simple adaptations of authentic recipes from outstanding European chefs.

Lois Goulder did her undergraduate work at Cornell University and the Northwestern University School of Journalism, and later received her Master's Degree in Education at Case Western Reserve University.

Her work experience is in the fields of advertising, public relations, education, and social service. Ms. Goulder's research skills and expertise in analyzing data were invaluable in organizing the vast amount of technical nutritional information that the authors compiled while writing these books: THE DELL COLOR-CODED LOW-SALT-LIVING GUIDE, and THE DELL COLOR-CODED LOW-FAT-LIVING GUIDE.